BRANDEN JACOBS-JENKINS

Branden Jacobs-Jenkins is a Brooklyn based playwright. Recent theatre credits include *Purpose* (Steppenwolf Theatre), *The Comeuppance* (Signature Theatre), *Girls* (Yale Rep), *Everybody* (Signature Theatre), *Gloria* (Vineyard Theatre; UK premiere: Hampstead Theatre), *Appropriate* (Obie Award; Signature Theatre; revived on Broadway in 2023; UK premiere: Donmar Warehouse) and *An Octoroon* (Obie Award; Soho Rep, Theatre for a New Audience; UK premiere: Orange Tree Theatre/National Theatre).

Honours include a USA Artists fellowship, a Guggenheim fellowship, the MacArthur fellowship, most promising playwright awards from both the Evening Standard and the London Critics' Circle, the Windham-Campbell Prize for Drama, and the inaugural Tennessee Williams Award. He teaches at Yale University.

Branden Jacobs-Jenkins

THE
COMEUPPANCE

NICK HERN BOOKS
London
www.nickhernbooks.co.uk

A Nick Hern Book

The Comeuppance first published in Great Britain as a paperback original in 2024 by Nick Hern Books Limited, The Glasshouse, 49a Goldhawk Road, London W12 8QP, by special arrangement with Theatre Communications Group, Inc., New York

The Comeuppance copyright © 2024 Branden Jacobs-Jenkins

Branden Jacobs-Jenkins has asserted his right to be identified as the author of this work

Cover image: art direction by Emilie Chen; photography by Vicki King

Designed and typeset by Nick Hern Books, London
Printed in the UK by Mimeo Ltd, Huntingdon, Cambridgeshire PE29 6XX

A CIP catalogue record for this book is available from the British Library

ISBN 978 1 83904 350 5

www.nickhernbooks.co.uk/environmental-policy

The Comeuppance was first performed at Signature Theatre, New York City, on 16 May 2023, with the following cast:

EMILIO   Caleb Eberhardt
URSULA   Brittany Bradford
CAITLIN   Susannah Flood
KRISTINA   Shannon Tyo
FRANCISCO   Bobby Moreno

Director   Eric Ting
Set Designer   Arnulfo Maldonado
Costume Designers   Jennifer Moeller
                          and Miriam Kelleher
Lighting Designer   Amith Chandrashaker
Sound Designer   Palmer Hefferan
Magic Designer   Skylar Fox
Intimacy Coordinator   Ann C. James

It received its UK premiere at the Almeida Theatre, London, on 6 April 2024, with the following cast:

EMILIO   Anthony Welsh
URSULA   Tamara Lawrance
CAITLIN   Yolanda Kettle
KRISTINA   Katie Leung
FRANCISCO   Ferdinand Kingsley

Director   Eric Ting
Set and Costume Designer   Arnulfo Maldonado
Lighting Designer   Natasha Chivers
Sound Designer   Emma Laxton
Magic Designers   Skylar Fox
                              and Will Houstoun
Intimacy Coordinator   Asha Jennings-Grant
Casting Director   Jatinder Chera
Dialect Coach   Rebecca Clark Carey
Assistant Director   Dubheasa Lanipekun

Characters

EMILIO
URSULA
CAITLIN
KRISTINA
FRANCISCO

SIMON

Note on the Text

A forward slash (/) indicates the point at which the next speaker interrupts.

This text went to press before the end of rehearsals and so may differ slightly from the play as performed.

1.

It is fall in the year of our Lord 2022. Somewhere in Prince George's County, Maryland. EMILIO *stands on a porch, staring into his phone, before he transforms into* DEATH.

DEATH. Oh, hello there… You and I, we have met before, though you may not recognize me. People have a tendency to see me once and try hard to forget it ever happened – though that never works – not for very long. Perhaps you know me by one of my many names? Mikhail? Azrael? Malakh ha Mavet? Muut? Mot? Anguta? Hine-nui-te-pō? Ankou? Anubis? Amokye? Ogbunabali? Owuo? Nāzi'āt? Nāshiṭāt? Yama? Tarakeshwara? Jeoseung Saja? Shinigami? Nasirdin? Sejadin? Hei Wuchang? Bai Wuchang? Wuluwaid? No…? Well those are only a handful of some in living memory… In any case, I should go out on a limb here and assume that no one present is familiar with the term 'psychopomp?' Which is fine. So you may call me, in the meantime, Death.

Hears something, notices URSULA *entering.*

Oops. Excuse me. What is this?

EMILIO *becomes* EMILIO *again as* URSULA, *stepping very carefully, emerges from the house with two drinks. She has an eyepatch over one eye.*

URSULA. Emilio?

EMILIO (*distracted*). Right here…

URSULA. You're going to have to come take it from me because –

EMILIO, hearing her, finally looks up from his phone, instantly stricken. He leaps up to take the drink from her.

EMILIO. Oh, shit, sorry – / I was texting with Simon –

URSULA. You know. Depth perception. Don't apologize. What's going on with Simon?

EMILIO. I think he just fucking cancelled?

EMILIO *calls* SIMON *on his phone and listens to it ring.*

URSULA. Oh no! That's disappointing...

EMILIO. Apparently he just got some big last-minute assignment about AI or something? Should we be worried? Is AI awake?

Beat.

He's not picking up...

(*Leaves a voicemail.*) Simon. What the fuck? I'm standing here on Ursula's porch with Ursula and she just used the word 'disappointing.' You cannot leave us hanging like this! Call us back!

Hangs up.

How the fuck are you going to cancel? This whole thing was your idea?

URSULA. What was?

EMILIO. This pre-game.

URSULA. I thought it was Kristina's idea?

EMILIO. No. The limo was Kristina's idea. It was just supposed to be a pre-reunion reunion and then Kristina Kristina'd it.

URSULA. I guess she always loved a limo.

EMILIO. Yeah, I sort of forgot they even existed. I haven't been in one since high school.

URSULA. You know, no one told me you were all coming by until yesterday.

EMILIO. It sounds like this came together super fast. And I think the idea we're going for is full-on nostalgia and your house was the prom house.

URSULA. The idea better not be trying to convince me to come, because I've already told Caitlin and Kristina it's not happening.

EMILIO (*hands up*). I don't know nothing about that. I just happened to be in the States for work. That's how I was guilted into coming down.

URSULA. Where are you staying while you're here?

EMILIO. Uh, The Mandarin?

URSULA. Oh? Fancy!

EMILIO. I had points, I had points! And it's just for the night. I go back to Manhattan tomorrow morning –

URSULA. For the biennial! How exciting.

EMILIO. That's right. And then Wednesday I fly home…

URSULA. To your little baby!

EMILIO. Yeah…

URSULA. She is so cute…

Beat.

How long has it been since you've been back here? Back in the DMV?

EMILIO. God, I don't know. My parents retired to Atlanta, so I'm haven't been back in DC since… maybe Kristina's wedding?

URSULA. Kristina's wedding is the last time you saw everyone?

EMILIO. Yes. I mean, Simon randomly came to a thing I had in London. That's how we reconnected. I guess he was there for work. Then there were those Zoom happy hours he organized during COVID. The ones I could make at least.

URSULA. Those were fun. Those were the early days.

EMILIO. Yeah. I've even begun to feel sort of nostalgic about the whole thing… But I hadn't heard from anyone in years until he started that group text… This is actually my first reunion ever.

Beat.

This whole thing is going to be weird, isn't it?

URSULA. The last few I went to were pretty weird.

EMILIO. In German, there are words for feelings that don't exist in English. Like the feelings exist, but only Germans were anal enough to name them. Like *Schadenfreude*. You know that one.

URSULA. Remind me?

EMILIO. It's sort of like, uh, finding joy in other people's misery. Or *Fernweh*, which is like the opposite of homesickness. It's like longing to be far away from where you are. *Torschlusspanik*. That's a good one. It literally translates into 'door closing panic.' It's like a fear that, as you get older, like all kind of doors are closing on you, like all these missed opportunities slipping away into oblivion.

URSULA....Are Germans okay!? These are so depressing.

EMILIO. There's *Kuddelmuddel*, that's a fun one, which is like... a totally chaotic situation. Like a shitstorm. Actually, shitstorm is pretty close. Anyway, I keep looking for a word to describe this specific feeling of dread that comes with attending your twentieth high-school reunion.

They drink.

URSULA. I like *Kuddelmuddel*. If you're worried, you can always be like me and not go. We could just hang out here all night.

EMILIO. That is a very tempting offer. Thank you.

URSULA. Do you think it's okay to keep everything out here? Do you think people will mind?

EMILIO (*shrugs*). Of course not. It's your house.

URSULA. There's not that much space inside and I get nervous about things being moved around –

EMILIO. Ursula, it's not a problem. Everyone will understand. This was super last-minute.

URSULA. And I figure it was a nice enough night –

EMILIO. It's perfect.

Sips the drink, impressed.

Man, this is delicious. I have to be careful.

URSULA. It's jungle juice –

EMILIO. No it's not!?

URSULA. But like a fancy adult spin on jungle juice. The secret is watermelon muddle. Shh!

EMILIO. Okay, shhh!

URSULA. I took these mixology classes during COVID, did I tell you?

EMILIO. No. During COVID?

URSULA. Yeah, like online. After Grandma died, I thought maybe I'd try bartending, but then you know...

She gestures to her eye.

EMILIO. What do you mean?

URSULA. No depth perception means you can't tell how far things are away from each other – or how far I am away from anything. Suddenly, everything's just like... a picture in a book somehow. So it makes pouring things difficult.

EMILIO. No kidding.

URSULA. Yeah, the things you take for granted... I also feel very aware that eyes are just like... portholes into... I want to say 'life' but it's really whatever... this is.

Gestures in front of her. Beat.

Anyway, so now I just have this weird, kind of sad hobby.

EMILIO. Do you have someone helping you?

URSULA. There's this woman who comes through a few times a week. She's nice.

Beat.

I'm going to sit down. Do you want to sit down?

EMILIO. Yes, let's do it.

The phone in his hand makes a sound.

Actually wait you know what? Can I charge this somewhere? I'm literally on like six percent.

URSULA. Oh, sure. There's one right in this front room here.

EMILIO *disappears inside to charge his phone.* URSULA *sits down with extreme care and rests her eyes for split second before* DEATH *inhabits her form.*

DEATH. Hi, again. You'll have to pardon me. I come and go. I get shy. Historically, I've been rarely met with anything other than fear or anger or regret and, as I'm sure you can imagine, that sort of energy gets... taxing. So I chose long ago to abandon any material form of my own and err on the side of the covert. I prefer now to move in and out of whatever vessel inspires me because, when I'm not working, I, like you, am a watcher. I like to watch. Sometimes I am in a tree. Sometimes in a rock. In a spider. In her web. The pollen in the air. A plant. A banister. That swing – I've been that, too. Each form offering its own... pleasures? Powers? Benefits? For instance, I inhabit a body like this if my desire is to speak and, if I have one weakness... it's for gossip. I suspect you share it?... I don't know what it is, but I find all creatures so interesting, their idiosyncracies, their interiorities, their secrets. Their stories. These machines of will. And, like any good gossip, I'm always wanting to talk but, you know, finding the right listeners can be a challenge. So you should know you are very special.

Hears the sound of a car pulling up.

Who is that?... Oh, I know her...

A door closes, an electronic lock beeps, and CAITLIN *emerges.*

CAITLIN. Ursula!

URSULA. Hiii.

CAITLIN. What are you doing outside? It's freezing!

URSULA. It's not that cold. Is it? I thought we could do this on the porch.

Beat.

CAITLIN. Oh... Okay! That's okay! Am I the first one here?

URSULA. Emilio is inside charging his phone.

CAITLIN. Oh, wow. Okay. I brought snacks!

Kisses URSULA *on the cheek.*

Hi, honey. How are you feeling?

URSULA. I'm feeling fine.

CAITLIN. Great! Then you can come!

URSULA. I'm not coming.

CAITLIN. Ursula, you only get one twentieth reunion and I really think you're cheating yourself out of something special. Think of all the people who want to see you!

URSULA. I don't want to be uncomfortable.

CAITLIN. Why would you be uncomfortable? It's just an eyepatch! There's going to be way worse accessories on display. And we're all going to be there! M.E.R.G.E.!

URSULA. I thought Simon just cancelled?

CAITLIN (*looking at her phone*). He did?

EMILIO (*off*). Am I hearing Caitlin?

URSULA. You are!

(*To* CAITLIN.) Listen, seeing everyone here is going to be enough but thank you.

EMILIO *emerges from the house.*

EMILIO. Hey!

CAITLIN. Hi, stranger!

They embrace.

EMILIO. Wow, this is weird. This is going to be so weird.

URSULA. Do you want a drink, Caitlin?

CAITLIN. Yes. Thank you!

URSULA *gets up, goes inside to make* CAITLIN *a drink.*

Hi!

EMILIO. Hi!

CAITLIN. I can't believe I haven't seen you since Kristina's wedding.

EMILIO. Me, neither. Fifteen years? What the full fuck?

CAITLIN. You look great.

EMILIO. Thanks. You, too.

CAITLIN. So we're doing this outside?

EMILIO. I think she's worried about people moving things around in there.

CAITLIN. That makes sense.

Beat.

Is this your first time seeing her since she lost the – ?

EMILIO. Yeah…

CAITLIN. It's a little crazy, right? We have got to get her to come to the reunion – get her out of the house. She's basically, like, become a shut-in. Her grandmother passed like right before the quarantine and then she was just all alone in the house and then lockdown happened and then she freaking goes blind and it's horrible. I'm afraid if we don't, you know, try, she'll never, you know, re-engage or something. You know what I mean? She has had like truly the worst pandemic ever – except for people who actually, you know… died. Anyway. This is going to be fun…

Beat.

How was your COVID? I don't even remember what they did over there.

EMILIO. Um. It was still a thing in Europe. Ironically, I got a ton of work done. I had a kid.

CAITLIN. Oh my God, wait! What? When?

EMILIO. Five months ago. Her name is Alena. (*Pronounced: AH-lin-ah.*)

CAITLIN. Way to bury the lede!

Struggling with pronounciation.

Olin-na?

EMILIO. Uh, yes. It's basically Alena. But German. My partner is German.

CAITLIN. Oh, right. Berlin is in Germany.

EMILIO. That's right.

CAITLIN. Oh my God! Congratulations!? Gosh, how long have you been out there now?

EMILIO. Thirteen years. But it might be about time to move back. We'll see.

CAITLIN. That would be fun. Do you have pictures?

EMILIO. Oh! Yes!

Reaching for phone.

Wait, my phone is charging. Let me go grab it.

(*Heading inside.*) How are your... kids...?

EMILIO *runs inside to grab the phone.*

CAITLIN (*shouting*). Good! They're good! Um, Brock just started law school at Madison, which is insane! And Olivia is a junior at UVA!

EMILIO (*off*). Oh, wow.

URSULA *emerges again with a drink, some snacks.*

URSULA. Here we go...

CAITLIN. Over here. Thank you, Ursula!

CAITLIN *takes the drink.* EMILIO *re-emerges with his phone, goes to show* CAITLIN.

EMILIO. Here she is...

CAITLIN. Oh my God, no! No!... She's beautiful...

EMILIO. Thanks. Made her myself. I mean, with help.

CAITLIN. Ursula, did you know Emilio had a kid?

URSULA. He just told me.

CAITLIN. Did you bring her with you?

EMILIO. No, she's back in Germany. She's only five months old.

CAITLIN. If I had known, I would have brought a gift. Congratulations...

CAITLIN *hands the phone back.*

EMILIO. Thanks.

CAITLIN *takes a sip.*

CAITLIN. Mm! Ursula!

URSULA. It's jungle juice.

CAITLIN. Jungle juice!? Okay?!

Sips, then –

(*To* EMILIO.) Mm, did Ursula tell you she took some mixology classes over the pandemic?

EMILIO. She did…

CAITLIN. I was trying to tell her she should really think about, you know, doing something with those classes.

URSULA. Blind bartenders are not a thing.

CAITLIN. That doesn't have to be true. Michael and I were in London a few years ago and we went to this really interesting restaurant – I can't remember what it's called but it's pitch black and it's supposed to approximate the experience of being visually impaired and all of the servers and the chefs and everything are visually impaired and it was just so interesting. And I feel like there's something there. Like wouldn't it be cool if there was a speakeasy-type thing that was pitch dark and you had, you know, a bartender who was visually impaired serving your drinks? I mean, I just think that would be so interesting.

Beat.

EMILIO. Do you remember that thing we used to do if someone was rambling?

URSULA. Oh my God, yes.

(*Pretending to snap her own neck.*) KRK.

EMILIO *laughs.*

CAITLIN.…Are you suggesting that I was just rambling?

EMILIO (*lying*). No, of course not… I was just reminded…

URSULA. Was it if you were rambling or if you were, like, harshing the buzz?

EMILIO. It was rambling. I'm pretty sure I invented the joke.

CAITLIN. Anyway! I can't believe Simon cancelled?

EMILIO. I know, so annoying. But he's offered to cover for the whole limo.

CAITLIN. Ugh, the limo.

EMILIO. Wait, you hate the limo?!

CAITLIN. Of course I hate the fucking limo! It's embarrassing!

EMILIO. The limo? No! It's funny!

CAITLIN. What? How?

EMILIO. Because in high school, every stupid prom, every homecoming, we were always randomly showing up in a limo like somehow it was a thing that people did in real life.

CAITLIN. But we're not teenagers anymore. Now we're just adults showing up in a limo.

EMILIO. But isn't the point of this dumb event reliving high school for the night? I think people will think it's funny. Maybe it is a little conceptual.

CAITLIN. 'Conceptual?' What does that mean?

EMILIO. Don't worry about it. Listen: it's just a little nostalgia.

Beat.

CAITLIN. Well, you don't still live around these people. I do...

EMILIO. So?

CAITLIN. So, for some of us, it may not be in our best interest to show up looking like shitheads.

EMILIO. Okay, well talk to Kristina. Though don't people already think you're a shithead by association?

CAITLIN. Why?

EMILIO. Because of your husband?

Beat, as CAITLIN *is stung.*

Wait, I'm joking. I'm sorry. I haven't been back in a – Can you still not joke about January Sixth? Are people still scared?

URSULA....Do you need a refill, E?

EMILIO. Yes, please.

URSULA *takes* EMILIO *'s cup, going back inside.*

Are you really insulted? I'm sorry –

CAITLIN. I just want to be mindful of other people's financial situations – like not everyone can afford a limo. And Michael was not in the group that actually *stormed* the Capitol. And, as you well know, he and I don't necessarily share the same politics…

EMILIO. I'm sure if you wanted to drive yourself, it wouldn't be a big deal.

CAITLIN. It's fine. Plus you're right. I don't want to ruin Kristina's night. I think she's actually very excited about it. Speaking of: where the eff is she?

EMILIO. Are you and Kristina still close?

CAITLIN. Uh, sort of? COVID's made things a little weird.

EMILIO. How so?

CAITLIN. Being a doctor during the pandemic seems to have not been the greatest experience? She's definitely, like, been through some shit and I think she may have developed a drinking problem as a result?

EMILIO. What?

CAITLIN. But I'm not sure? You'll have to tell me when you see her. The last couple of times we met up for happy hour, she sort of like drank so much she… blacked out?… As a grown woman?… And I was sort of like, 'Huh…' You know how there's like this behavior that you can get away with in your twenties and everyone's like, 'Oh *xyz* is so fun.' But then you turn this corner and suddenly it's like, 'Oh she has a problem.' That's kind of where I am with Kristina. I'm like, 'Am I supposed to say something?' But also she's a doctor so, like, wouldn't she know better than me? But also she spent lockdown trapped in a house with Cameron and their five kids, so who am I to judge? Watching that was like… the beginning of a podcast about murder.

EMILIO. It's funny to think there's a bizarro multiverse in which she and I are still together.

CAITLIN. How long did you and Kristina 'date' or whatever? I forget.

EMILIO. Half of sophomore year and all of junior year?

Beat.

Five kids, though?

CAITLIN. I know. Catholicism.

EMILIO. You know, if I thought anyone was going to have a buttload of kids, it was going to be you...

CAITLIN. I have kids.

EMILIO. I mean, like kids of your own. How did Michael talk you out of that?

CAITLIN. Uh, no one talked me out of anything. It just never happened.

DEATH *inhabits the form of* CAITLIN.

DEATH. Actually – and not to make this moment about me – what happened was, well... one, two, three, four miscarriages over the course of as many years? If not a little less. After a while, it was difficult to keep track. And if you're not careful, the same small tragedies repeated again and again begin to take on a new shape, begin to stack up into something larger – a bigger story you start telling yourself. The story of your curse. When, honestly, what I do is not something anyone *deserves.*

Caitlin doesn't really talk about it much, obviously, because – after the first or second, it started to feel like a character flaw. Or at least that's how her husband made her feel about it – though he enjoys his own kids from a previous marriage. He made her stop. Her nerviness was getting to be too much for him. It was turning her into a whiner. It was making her seem unattractive. And who needs their husband thinking that? And there are worse things than a dead fetus. For instance: a dead baby. For instance: a dead toddler. With a positive enough mindset, you might even find a way to consider yourself lucky.

Meanwhile, she's still got her figure. Nice skin. Good teeth. There is so much to admire about the human body. Especially at this age, so noble, fighting its good fight against a certain... softening. Your cell-repair systems – my most ancient nemeses – are long broken down. You lose those at twenty-seven. Did you know that? Is anyone here twenty-seven?... From that point on, it's my game. Wrinkles. A little sag. A creaking in the joints. A misplaced word or two or several. From that point on, it's just me and you... and you... and you... and you... and you...

Anyway, let me stop –

CAITLIN *becomes* CAITLIN *again just as* URSULA *re-emerges with the refill.*

CAITLIN. Wait, Ursula! You know who I just heard is going to be there tonight?

URSULA. Who?

CAITLIN. Cindy Podolski.

URSULA. Oh my God! Not Cindy!

EMILIO. Who?

CAITLIN. Cindy Podolski!? Come on, you remember her? She was epileptic?

CAITLIN *takes out her phone, begins searching on some app.*

EMILIO. That's her identifying feature?!

URSULA. She had a full-on seizure on the dance floor sophomore homecoming and everyone didn't realize and formed a circle around her and were like, 'Go Cindy! Go Cindy!' It was terrible.

EMILIO. Wait, I do kind of remember that...

URSULA. It actually happened multiple times.

CAITLIN. I think she did it for the attention. There: I said it.

EMILIO. Are you saying she faked being epileptic?

CAITLIN. I'm saying it's suspicious that she kept going back to the dances. It's like returning to the scene of the crime.

URSULA. Is there going to be dancing tonight?

CAITLIN. There was at the fifteenth. Here she is.

CAITLIN, *having found Cindy's profile, hands her phone to*
EMILIO *to inspect.*

EMILIO. Oh, yeah… I remember her… She's coming from
Seattle? That's far.

CAITLIN. I think people are coming in from all over. I guess
twenty is a big number. Which is why you need to come,
Ursula! Don't you want to see Cindy seize again!?

URSULA. I'm good.

CAITLIN. But you went to the fifteenth and the tenth and the
fifth. It's going to be odd if you drop out. People are going to
think you're dead! I don't want to keep having to explain to
people that you're not dead!

EMILIO. How were those other reunions?

CAITLIN. They were fine. How come you never came?

EMILIO *continues scrolling through* CAITLIN*'s phone.*

EMILIO. I… don't know. I was still on Facebook at the time, so
I figured, like, 'Why bother?' We all knew what we looked
like, who had kids, who didn't have kids, who had what kind
of job. I just found the idea of gathering in some random two-
star Marriott to confirm all that just so tedious. I feel like
before Facebook, reunions were a real encounter with the
brutal beatdown of time. You just sort of showed up and had
no idea who would be there or how fucked up they would look
and then you realized that maybe you looked a little fucked up
too and every encounter was like a whole dark ritual of the
soul where each party was confronted by the specter of their
own mortality, just like, 'Oh shit!' I don't know. You know?

Beat.

CAITLIN. I… thought it was just fun to see people…

URSULA. So what's so different now, Emilio?

EMILIO. What do you mean?

URSULA. You're going tonight?

EMILIO. Uh, I'm not on Facebook anymore –

CAITLIN *remembers* EMILIO *still has her phone.*

CAITLIN. Wait – what are you doing with my phone?

EMILIO. I'm looking at who else you follow – Oh my God, is this Huey Michael Lewis?

URSULA. Awww, Huey Michael Lewis!

EMILIO. I have not thought about this guy since the oughties… Didn't he used to wear a diaper or something?

URSULA. He did not wear a diaper. He just had a big ass.

EMILIO. This is a lot of pictures of him with guns. And trucks… Oh there's him with a gun in front of a truck… And that's a tank. He's military?

CAITLIN. Was.

EMILIO. Wait, how are you friends with Huey Michael Lewis?

CAITLIN. I don't know. He just added me one day.

EMILIO. And you accepted?

CAITLIN. Yes? Why not? Give me my phone back!

CAITLIN *snatches her phone back. Beat, as everyone drinks.*

EMILIO. God, guys, remember Columbine?

Beat.

CAITLIN. Uh, yeah?… What?!

EMILIO. Man, compared to now it feel almost… like quaint – but remember how everyone was so much nicer to Huey afterwards? Like everyone was afraid of him?

CAITLIN. I think that was just you.

EMILIO. No, it was not just me! People were scared! He was totally Columbine… ey? So Columbiney.

URSULA. 'Columbiney?'

EMILIO. You know: spookily quiet? Kind of a recluse? Physically sort of… elven? And, I mean, he was JROTC, which was like free revenge-training for baby psychopaths. Like, oh my God, Ryan Morgan? Do you remember him? And that guy with the birthmark on his face – Frankie… Something. Their energy was way too dark for teenagers. And they were all in rifle club together. I mean, why was there a rifle club at our school? Like, why would you give these people access to guns? The fact you're even fake-training for a life in the military at that age clearly means there's something wrong with you.

CAITLIN. Half of our friends were in / JROTC – ?

EMILIO. Yeah, but that's not the same thing. Ursula only did it for a year and only for the little discount on tuition they gave you and Kristina's dad is a sergeant or whatever so she was really born into it – / *indoctrinated* –

CAITLIN. And Paco.

EMILIO. Okay, and Paco, but I mean, come on, hello – case in point: Paco was psychotic.

CAITLIN. Paco was not *psychotic*?

EMILIO. Caitlin, are you kidding me? Paco had obvious emotional problems. Look at the way he treated you. Though, what am I even talking about? Your profound lack of boundaries back then didn't exactly help.

CAITLIN. Excuse me?

EMILIO. Oh, come on… You know your whole obsession in high school with having a boyfriend? It just led you into these bad situations with these like messed-up, manipulative Big Chief Dickhead-types and Paco was like – ugh, he was like the platonic form of this asshole. Like, he was always making you feel like shit for not doing the things he wanted you to do so then you'd do them but then he'd just basically ignore you afterwards and you'd be like crying all through lunch period and refusing to eat until everyone would have to convince you to break up but then he'd be like running around like emotionally punching lockers for the rest of the day until you'd go back to him so you could feel… needed I guess. The cycle would just go on and on and on. But, you know, I suppose no one got enough attention at home or whatever.

(*Off* CAITLIN*'s reaction.*) What? We've definitely talked about this? Like a million years ago? Do you not remember this?

Beat.

CAITLIN. The point is Huey Michael Lewis didn't shoot up the school. He actually joined the military, which was the point of JROTC –

EMILIO. Okay.

CAITLIN. And so did Kristina, who did actual ROTC in college –

EMILIO. Right, to pay for med school, and now she's a doctor, / so that's cheating –

CAITLIN. And Paco –

EMILIO. Okay…?

CAITLIN. And Frankie Martinez and Ryan Marshall actually both served, too, you know.

EMILIO. Really?

CAITLIN. Yeah, Ryan did like three tours of Afghanistan. And Frankie was in Baghdad with Paco for a while actually. The same platoon or whatever.

EMILIO. Okay, Caitlin, so the military continued to be a home for an endless parade of formerly unstable youth. How is that news? I was just talking about Columbine.

Beat.

How do you know all this? You follow them on Instagram, too?

CAITLIN. What if I am?

EMILIO. I don't know. You weren't friends with any of these people in high school.

CAITLIN. What does that have to do with anything? You just add people on Instagram?! Bloop bloop / bloop follow back follow back bloop – !

EMILIO. Why are you screaming at me?

CAITLIN. Because you're suddenly trying to tell me who I can and who I can't be friends with on Instagram!

EMILIO. Whoa, whoa, whoa, okay, okay! Chill.

Beat.

CAITLIN. Paco was almost killed over there. Are you aware of this?

EMILIO. No?

CAITLIN. He was in some sort of ambush situation. He was in a truck behind some truck that hit one of those IED things and he only survived because the one he was in turned over and he was basically crushed inside while the rest of them, you know, fought off... the insurgents or whatever. But he broke both his legs, had all these – what do you call it? – shrapnel wounds. Couldn't walk for months. Half of his friends died and he was just trapped there listening to it happen.

EMILIO. Jesus... When was this?

CAITLIN. 2010? 2011? A while ago. Anyway, I found out about that and I reached out back then. I wrote him little messages or whatever on Facebook and, when we were going back and forth, he told me there were a lot of guys over there who didn't have anyone writing to them and I started feeling guilty for some reason and, I don't know, one day I just sort of woke up in the middle of the night and friended everybody in our class who I knew or heard was over there and wrote them little notes too and I guess when everything switched over to Instagram they migrated with me. So that's why I'm friends with all those guys. Alright?

Beat.

Where is Kristina?

EMILIO. How long were you talking to Paco?

CAITLIN. I don't know. A few years?

EMILIO. Are you still in touch?

CAITLIN. Uh, not really. He moved out to California when he came back. Kristina told me he was finishing his degree. We sort of lost touch. I don't know if he even checks his messages anymore. He never posts.

EMILIO. That's so weird.

CAITLIN. How is that weird?

EMILIO. I don't know. I guess I remember things between you two ending on a gross note.

CAITLIN. That was high school.

EMILIO. I'm just surprised.

CAITLIN (*after a beat*). He actually used to ask about you a lot – about how you were doing.

EMILIO. Why?

CAITLIN. Because I guess he thought he was your friend?

EMILIO. Uh, well, he wasn't. He was your boyfriend. And a piece of shit to me.

CAITLIN. He only gave you a hard time because you were dating Kristina and that was his cousin.

URSULA. Do you guys / want to smoke some pot?

EMILIO. Oh, give me a break – what?

CAITLIN. What?

URSULA. What?

EMILIO. No, what did you say?

URSULA. I said do you guys want to smoke pot?

Beat.

I'm going to switch over. Be right back.

URSULA *exits.* CAITLIN *and* EMILIO *exchange looks.*

EMILIO. Is this okay?

CAITLIN. I think so? Maybe she has a prescription?

EMILIO. For what? Being blind in one eye? That's not a thing.

CAITLIN. Well, it's legal now.

EMILIO. Right.

CAITLIN. And, honestly, Ursula's always secretly sort of been a huge pothead, I think. She and her grandma both.

EMILIO. What?

CAITLIN. Back when she was alive, they would just like wake up and smoke pot all day.

URSULA *re-emerges with a cute little box.*

EMILIO. Ursula, confirm or deny: you and Grandma were wake-and-bakers?

URSULA (*shoots a glance at* CAITLIN). She was dying of like fifteen cancers. She had a prescription. She wanted company. What are you gonna do? Call the cops? She's dead.

EMILIO. You smoked pot with Grandma!?

URSULA. Of course I smoked pot with my grandmother! You remember that woman! She was insane. It was the only way we could deal with each other by the end.

EMILIO. Well, what's your excuse now?

URSULA. My excuse is, if I have another drink, I may go into diabetic shock. Now do you want some or no?

EMILIO. I'll smoke a little.

CAITLIN. Did you guys smoke weed in high school?

URSULA. No. Not really. Did you?

CAITLIN. No.

EMILIO. I think senior year I, like, 'experimented.' But I was too worried about my grades.

URSULA. Same.

CAITLIN. Same.

Beat.

EMILIO. Man, why were we just… nerd city?

URSULA *becomes* DEATH.

DEATH. I'd like to counteract an impression I fear I might have left you with. Do not get the impression that I am some sort of misanthrope. I am quite friendly. In fact, I recognized a few of you out there, in the dark. And I think some would argue that knowing me comes with certain benefits. Certain sensitivities and insights, a lucidity, a greater patience for mystery, a sense of humor. For example, Ursula. She has known me quite intimately for some time now, mostly through her grandmother's extended battles with the fickleness of the human cell. But my actual relationship with Ursula goes as far back as when she was a newborn. Her mother, the day after Ursula's delivery, stood up too quickly from her hospital bed, fell and cracked her head against the corner of a radiator. She died instantly but bled and bled and bled and the sight of all that blood sent her father running, never to return, too worried he might not ever look at his daughter and feel anything other than grief. So this is why her grandmother had to raise her.

Of course, when asked about the arrangement, you never lead with the details. You say simply, 'My mother died.' Which inevitably leads to the question 'When?' To which Ursula must reply, 'Shortly after I was born.' Then there's usually this pause as they wonder if she might be the culprit. Then comes the dreaded '…How?' And, depending on the questioner, Ursula will or won't make a joke I never tire of. She goes, 'Like this – '

Mimes dying, laughs.

Hilarious. Because truly what difference does it make? They want to know but they really don't and, when you're in a situation like hers, you learn very early about the average person's capacity for avoiding those who seem to carry my mark. Everyone treats you differently. So, up close and personal with the power of fear, its absurdity, you develop a real sense of humor about things – about people. About life. And look at her. I think she's wonderful. I'm allowed to think people are wonderful.

URSULA *becomes* URSULA *again.*

CAITLIN (*checking the time*). What is taking Kristina so long!? That limo is going to be here soon.

URSULA *lights up, smokes, and then passes the enormous joint to* EMILIO.

EMILIO. This is for two people?

URSULA. Is that not enough?

EMILIO. Ursula, this J is enormous!

URSULA. Well, it's not that strong, I think.

EMILIO. Caitlin, you have to have some of this or I'm not going to make it to the reunion.

CAITLIN. I don't want to show up to our reunion stoned!

EMILIO. Come on. Nobody cares you're married to an ex-cop. Nobody's going to make you pee into a cup. Just have a little bit. Ursula just said it wasn't that strong.

The phone in his hand makes a noise.

Shit. I keep forgetting about my phone. Here!

EMILIO *hands the joint to* CAITLIN *who, after a small hesitation, takes it, and he runs back inside to charge his phone.* CAITLIN *tokes a little, coughs, carefully passes it to* URSULA.

CAITLIN. Can you believe Emilio has a kid?

URSULA. I know?!

CAITLIN. Who is his partner?

URSULA. I don't know.

CAITLIN. Wow. I wonder how they did it. That sort of thing can be so expensive. Is he, like, rich now?

URSULA. He's staying at The Mandarin.

EMILIO *re-enters.*

EMILIO. What are you gossiping about?

URSULA. You. Hey, are you rich?

EMILIO. Um, no. I'm still fucking DJing to pay bills.

URSULA. Okay, then how did you have your kid?

CAITLIN. Yeah!

EMILIO. What do you mean how did I have her?

URSULA. How did, you know, how did you do it?

EMILIO. I... impregnated my partner?

Beat.

URSULA. Oh! Okay!

Beat.

CAITLIN. Oh! Your partner is… female…

EMILIO. Yes…

CAITLIN. I, okay. Wow. Because you used the word 'partner' and I wasn't… okay. Okay. What's her name?

EMILIO. Annika…

CAITLIN. / Oh!

URSULA. So pretty!

EMILIO. I…

CAITLIN. What?

EMILIO. I can't help but notice how… surprised you acted when I told you that my partner was a woman.

URSULA. Oh, no, no –

CAITLIN. It's not like we wouldn't accept you no matter what.

EMILIO. But why would I just like… suddenly be gay?

CAITLIN. Well, I mean, um…

EMILIO. I'm sorry but am I learning right now that you thought I was gay in high school?

CAITLIN. I don't know! You were always… really into art!

EMILIO. I was – I'm an artist!

CAITLIN. Exactly. But you didn't play any sports in high school. You were really neat. And so stylish!

EMILIO. What? But I actually had a girlfriend! Who you knew!

CAITLIN. Yeah, but you guys never did anything!

EMILIO. What? Who told you that?

URSULA*'s cellphone rings.*

CAITLIN. Kristina did. She said, when you were dating, you wouldn't even let her give you a handjob.

EMILIO. Are you kidding? What? She's the one who told me she was afraid to blow me because she didn't like the idea of her mouth that close to somebody's asshole!

URSULA (*picking up*). Speaking of – Hey Kristina... Yeah, we're here... Yes, I heard. Everyone's annoyed at him... / Okay... Yeah, just have them pull in around the corner.

She laughs at something KRISTINA *says.*

Okay. Bye.

CAITLIN. What?

EMILIO. She had like a huge thing about butts. Remember how she would break down into tears if she smelled a fart? She was like OCD. She wouldn't even let me finger her because she lived in constant fear of yeast infections.

CAITLIN. But why didn't you let her give you a handjob?

EMILIO. Because I didn't want a fucking handjob! And she doesn't get to give me a handjob if I can't finger her. That doesn't seem fair!

CAITLIN. Well, you were the only guy in school keeping track.

EMILIO. Yeah, you would know, wouldn't you...

Beat.

CAITLIN. Also Paco and I always thought you had a crush on Simon. The way you guys were like attached at the hip –

EMILIO. What the fuck are you – I did not have a crush on Simon!

CAITLIN. Okay, well, just calm down. You're really getting a little over-defensive about this for a straight guy.

EMILIO. Oh that's rich. Coming from the in-house expert here on the psychology of the straight man. Tell me how I should be acting. Should I be more like your dreamy blue-lives-matter-enthusiast COVID-truther of a husband telling you who to vote for? Or maybe I should have knocked you up a million times and joined the Marines and nearly get blown up and become your fucking penpal because I'm so emotionally stunted? God forbid I was the guy driving you to every Planned Parenthood in the tri-state area. That is apparently reserved for the gay best friend, right? Jesus... Fuck Kristina.

Beat, as CAITLIN *is stung.* EMILIO *takes a drink. Then* URSULA *puts down her drink, carefully feels her way over to* EMILIO *and pretends to break his neck.*

URSULA. KRRRK!

EMILIO almost spits up his drink. CAITLIN*'s jaw falls open. Everyone is delighted.*

EMILIO. Oh my God –

CAITLIN. L. O. L. Ursula.

EMILIO. Wait, first of all, I didn't deserve that. You didn't even use it right –

URSULA. Yes, I did.

EMILIO. No, you didn't. I wasn't rambling!

URSULA. You were harshing the buzz!

EMILIO. That's not what it's for!

CAITLIN. Whatever. The point is you do it to make someone shut up. Thank you, Ursula!

EMILIO. Whatever. Oh wait do you remember this one?

Pretends to stab CAITLIN *in the stomach and lower her to the ground.*

Shhhh, shhhh, shhhh, shhhh, shhhh!

CAITLIN. What was wrong with us?

The sound of a horn honking crazily as a car drives by.

KRISTINA (*off*). HAY WHORES!

URSULA. Is that Kristina?

CAITLIN. Yes. Who's she with? Is that Cameron?

EMILIO. Wait. You guys I just got an idea.

CAITLIN. What?

EMILIO. We should totally moon Kristina. It'll freak her out.

CAITLIN. Why would we moon Kristina? That doesn't make any sense.

EMILIO. Because it'll freak her out!

URSULA. But I thought you only mooned people from the car.

EMILIO. Okay, why are you guys being so technical? We just pull our fucking pants down and moon her as she walks up! It'll be funny.

CAITLIN. Emilio, why would pulling our pants down be funny!?

EMILIO. Because Kristina's a fucking prude and a gossip with a buttphobia and we haven't fucking seen each other in a long – Fuck you guys. I'm mooning her.

EMILIO *gets up on the chair and pulls his pants down and moons the walkway.*

CAITLIN (*seeing who's coming*). Wait that's not... Cameron...

KRISTINA *comes walking up, following by* FRANCISCO. KRISTINA *is dressed in her dress greens.* FRANCISCO *is just dressed in a suit.* URSULA *greets them sincerely.* CAITLIN *is struck dumb by the sight of* FRANCISCO *while* EMILIO *just stands really still on the porch with his pants down.* KRISTINA *and* FRANCISCO *don't even really notice him until they're really close.*

KRISTINA. Hey, you guys!

URSULA. Kristina, you made... it.

CAITLIN. Oh my God...

EMILIO (*moving cheeks to make his buttocks sing*). 'Oh say can you see – by the dawn's early light – '

KRISTINA *is briefly stunned and appalled.*

FRANCISCO. Hey, I recognize that phat ass! Emilio?!

EMILIO *turns around, pulling his pants up, startled at the sound of* FRANCISCO*'s voice. Beat, in which he takes in* FRANCISCO *and* KRISTINA.

EMILIO. ...Paco... hello...

KRISTINA. Oh, right – surprise! Hi, Emilio...

FRANCISCO. You been working out? Look at that juicy cookie. Nom, nom, nom, no homo.

EMILIO. What is going on?

CAITLIN *crosses to hug* FRANCISCO.

CAITLIN (*hugging him*). Oh my God! What is happening right now?

FRANCISCO. I know! I'm back! And I definitely owe you like a thousand emails, sorry –

(*Hugging* CAITLIN.) But, man, a real-life hug! What?!

CAITLIN. You're... here?

KRISTINA. Paco's just moved back, you guys.

FRANCISCO. That's right. It's crazy! But look at everybody! Look at M.E.R.G.E.! And, holy crap, is this your grandmother's house, Ursula? I barely recognize it...

URSULA. Yes. My COVID project. I remodeled after she died a few year sago.

FRANCISCO. I heard. I'm sorry. But whoa! Isn't this where we took our prom pictures... Oh, shit... I was just looking at those photos...

EMILIO....I don't understand.

KRISTINA. Wait, let me back up: why are we mooning people? How drunk is everybody?

URSULA. Um, well, I made fancy jungle juice.

KRISTINA. Okay. Mama likey what she heary.

URSULA. I can make you one.

KRISTINA. Make me two so I can catch up.

URSULA. Paco, do you want one?

FRANCISCO. Thanks but I, uh, gotta abstain tonight. Though can I use your facilities?

URSULA. Of course you can. I'll show you where it is.

FRANCISCO. Love it. I also heard you got popped with the 'betes!? That sucks.

URSULA. Yeah...

FRANCISCO. Sweet patch though. No, really. Like a hot pirate. Oh shit, look at these posters!

They exit. Beat.

KRISTINA. It's alright that I brought him, right?

CAITLIN. Uh, sure –

KRISTINA. Okay, good. I should have given you a heads-up but it's just been complete madness since he got home like two days ago and when I finally saw him last night, I actually asked if he wanted to come with us to the reunion but he said no and this afternoon he texted me saying yes and then it was no and then it was yes. I think the reason he kept going back and forth about coming was because he knew you'd be here, Caitlin. I guess he feels bad because he hasn't written you or something? But I was like, 'She's not going to give a fuck! How long has it been since you've seen each other? She's going to be totally thrilled to see you.' Right?

CAITLIN. Right…

KRISTINA. Exactly. And I thought this would be good for him. He missed his own reunion last year I thought, 'Why not?' It would be fun to, you know, see people. Other than his mom, I mean. His friends – M.E.R.G.E.! Anyway, so I had to drive all the way out to Gaithersburg to get him, which is why I am so late, sorry, but I called the limo people and pushed it back by half an hour so we should be fine. Aren't we hyped about this limo!? I specifically requested a party limo! Remember party limos!?

EMILIO. Wait, he's coming to the reunion?

KRISTINA.…Uh, yes?

EMILIO. But he wasn't in our class…

KRISTINA. So? How the fuck are they going to know who anyone is? We'll just sneak him in. I mean now that Simon's fucking cancelled, maybe we'll just tell everyone he's Simon. Actually that's not a bad idea. Can you believe that asshole cancelled? Who cares if robots are learning to type or whatever? Caitlin, this dress is gorgeous…

CAITLIN. Thanks… Yours… too…?

KRISTINA. Ugh, LOL. No, they asked anyone who's ever served to show up in their dress blues for some sort of award ceremony. But now I am very much regretting it because the kids are at Grandma's and Cameron is at a goddamned dermasurgery conference in Minneapolis, so my MO tonight is to get my literal freak on. Actually, let me take this jacket off, in case somebody rides by and decides to get in my business because I've got pre-gaming to do.

She removes a layer.

Oh wait, where is my phone?

(*Shouting into the house.*) Paco, do you have my phone!?

FRANCISCO (*off*). Yeah! In my pocket!

KRISTINA. Okay, thanks!

(*To* CAITLIN *and* EMILIO.) I want to make sure we take a ton of pictures. Make Simon jealous. Actually, we should call that motherfucker and curse him out.

FRANCISCO (*off*). Wait, Kristina, can you come in here and help us for a second?

KRISTINA. Sure. BRB.

(*Half inside.*) Oh my God, why are you guys laughing? What's so funny?

KRISTINA *exits inside the house.*

CAITLIN. Oh no…

EMILIO. I know. What the fuck?!

CAITLIN. I'm too stoned for this. Oh no…

EMILIO. What does Kristina think she's doing? This is so inconsiderate.

CAITLIN. What?

EMILIO. I mean, what the fuck is she even talking about? 'M.E.R.G.E?' Paco was not even in M.E.R.G.E.

CAITLIN. Yes he was.

EMILIO. No he wasn't. Just because you dated doesn't make him a member of our group. She can't just hijack this and turn this into Paco's Welcome Home Party.

CAITLIN. Why? Because it was your Welcome Home Party!?

EMILIO. Uh, no, Caitlin?

Beat.

Wait, what just happened?

CAITLIN. What are you talking about?

EMILIO. Why are you suddenly acting so different?

CAITLIN. Because I'm high! Because you and Ursula made me do drugs!

EMILIO. Made you?

Beat.

Wait… I remember this…

CAITLIN. Remember what?

EMILIO. Your being… weird…

CAITLIN. Will you stop it? You are spiraling. Please just be nice.

EMILIO. Be nice? Do you not remember what this man did to you?

CAITLIN (*fake-shoots* EMILIO). Bang, bang, bang, pow, pow, pow!… Stop!

URSULA, KRISTINA, *and* FRANCISCO *return from the kitchen.* URSULA *has the full pitcher of jungle juice and extra cups.* KRISTINA *has two drinks for herself.* FRANCISCO *has a non-alcoholic drink for himself and a drink for* EMILIO. CAITLIN *steps away from* EMILIO, *as if nothing particularly weird has just happened.*

KRISTINA. Reeeeeeefills!

Everyone – except CAITLIN *and* EMILIO *– hands out their cups, sort of exchanging furtive glances.*

CAITLIN. Are those both really for you?

KRISTINA. No. One's for Simon. Glug glug, mind your beeswax!

URSULA. Here, Caitlin. I brought out the whole pitcher.

FRANCISCO (*handing* EMILIO *the drink*). This one's for you, buddy.

EMILIO (*dry*). Thanks…

KRISTINA. Should we make a toast?

FRANCISCO. We should! Toast! Toast! Toast!

Everyone raises their glasses except for EMILIO.

URSULA. What are we toasting to?

FRANCISCO. To M.E.R.G.E.!

EVERYONE (*except* EMILIO). To M.E.R.G.E.!

They all drink – except for EMILIO. FRANCISCO, KRISTINA, *and* URSULA *seem to notice.*

FRANCISCO. You not going to drink your drink?

EMILIO. I'm pacing myself.

FRANCISCO. It's bad luck after a toast, though –

EMILIO (*sets his drink aside*). It's okay. But thank you for your concern. Why aren't you drinking?

FRANCISCO. Oh, uh. I'm on some meds at the moment.

EMILIO. What kind of meds?

FRANCISCO. For minding your own business. You want some? Just kidding. I had some dental work done. It's just antibiotics.

URSULA. Paco just told me he was working in film.

CAITLIN. I didn't know that – !

FRANCISCO. Well, not in film. I was working on movie sets, but it didn't really pan out – though I did fill-in on a Fast and the Furious movie once working for craft services –

CAITLIN. / Oh –

URSULA. Oh wow –

KRISTINA. What is craft services?

EMILIO. He was a caterer –

FRANCISCO. Getting on crews is really competitive. The unions are crazy. A lot of assholes. But whatever. The West Coast wasn't really my vibe anyway. I don't know why they call it the Best Coast. Everything's always on fire and everyone just, like, accepts that as normal. Ha ha ha... Anyway, yeah, so it's been a weird few years, but I guess it's been a weird few years for everybody... But now I'm back! And, man, everyone looks exactly like they used to. It's wild. I guess you don't realize how much you miss people until you're back in the same room with them...

EMILIO. Paco, jog my memory: were you actually *in* M.E.R.G.E.?

FRANCISCO (*laughs*). What do you mean?

EMILIO. Were you, like, officially a Multi-Ethnic Reject? I recall you were like super popular?

FRANCISCO. I like to think I was just friends with everybody but, wait, was M.E.R.G.E. like an official thing? I thought that's just something you called yourself.

KRISTINA. / No –

EMILIO. Yes... Kristina, what are you talking about?

KRISTINA. We weren't actually, like, a gang, Emilio?

EMILIO. Huh?! Yes we were!

KRISTINA. Yeah, but like... ironically? We were just in all the same honors classes. We didn't do, like, gang stuff?

EMILIO. We went to every dance together. We are literally pre-gaming before our reunion together. That is gang stuff?!

FRANCISCO. What did M.E.R.G.E. stand for again?

URSULA. Multi-Ethnic Reject Group.

FRANCISCO. Oh. Does that spell 'Merge' or 'Merg?'

KRISTINA / EMILIO / URSULA. It's a soft G.

FRANCISCO (*trying it out*). Merg... g... g...

CAITLIN. I thought at some point we called it the Experience? Like the Multi-Ethnic Reject Group Experience?

EMILIO. Okay, but just to bring it back to the original question here, you weren't in M.E.R.G.E., right?

FRANCISCO. I guess not.

KRISTINA. He was an associate member. Through Caitlin.

EMILIO. Oh, okay, so we weren't a gang but there was an associate level?

KRISTINA. Wait, why are we talking about this?!

CAITLIN. Yeah, Emilio. Why are we talking about this?

Beat.

EMILIO. Because I'm trying to get the facts straight. I seem to have… very different, uh, memories than everyone else. I'm beginning to wonder if we even actually knew each other?

CAITLIN. Okay, you're being overdramatic.

URSULA *rushes over and embraces* EMILIO.

URSULA. Emilio is mad at us because we thought he was gay and he's not!

Beat.

KRISTINA. Oh.

FRANCISCO. Oh…?

Beat.

I've got a bunch of gay friends. They're awesome dudes.

EMILIO. Well, Paco, I'm not actually gay so there's no need to showcase your tolerance. Thank you. Kristina, seriously, did you actually think this when we were actually dating?

KRISTINA. Not at first, but then, you know, we never did anything.

EMILIO. Because you never wanted to do anything! You were a huge prude!

KRISTINA. I was the huge prude?

EMILIO. Yes! You were afraid of my asshole!

FRANCISCO. He's right, Kristina. You did have a butt thing in high school. / Wait is that why we were mooned?

KRISTINA. No, I didn't.

FRANCISCO. What the – Caitlin, you're nodding?

CAITLIN. Kristina, I feel any time I happened to mention someone had a cute butt or something you would always go like this.

CAITLIN *mimics a young* KRISTINA *in the throes of her phobia.*

KRISTINA. Because I was not an 'asswoman,' Caitlin.

FRANCISCO. And didn't the girls lacrosse team find out you had a butt thing and then they all threaten to fart on you during games every time you missed a goal or something? And so you got really paranoid and quit the team? Didn't that happen?

KRISTINA. I cared about hygiene, okay!? We were all going through fucking puberty. It was gross. People didn't know how to wipe their asses. People still don't know how to wipe their asses. It's an epidemic. I'm a doctor. I know this. And maybe, in high school, I wasn't super interested in contracting typhoid or fucking giardia because some idiot didn't have enough home training to wipe twice before he pulled up his nasty skivvies. And, meanwhile, as a doctor, let me just say I have had people die on my operating table and do you know what happens when you die? You shit yourself, okay? And who has to smell it? Me. Who has to deal with it? Me. So obviously I have grown tremendously in the interim so why don't we all just let this go. The past is the past and right now we're not talking about me. We're talking about Emilio! So, Emilio, you're not gay. That's amazing. How did we figure this out?

URSULA. Because Emilio had a baby.

KRISTINA. You did? When?

URSULA. Five months ago? Six?

KRISTINA. Oh my God, congratulations!

FRANCISCO. Whoa, yeah! Congrats!

Beat.

EMILIO. Why am I beginning to feel like I'm on a porch with a bunch of strangers all of a sudden?

CAITLIN. Emilio, what are you talking about?

EMILIO. If you guys thought I was some big gay, why did you never bring it up?

KRISTINA. Come on. You've been incommunicado since, like, my wedding.

CAITLIN. Yeah, and maybe you needed time and space to like figure yourself out... Being a gay in this community was probably very –

EMILIO. Okay, you can shut up.

KRISTINA. Whatever, Emilio! Now we know the truth! It's a different world now! It's not even that big of a deal! Now can I please see some baby pictures?

Beat, before EMILIO *exits to retrieve his phone. Everyone looks at each other.*

FRANCISCO. I forgot you guys dated.

KRISTINA. Yeah... Man, I suddenly feel... I feel, uh, I want to say déjà vu but maybe what I really mean is I feel something very ancient returning...

URSULA. Guys, are we being a little mean?

KRISTINA. Oh come on, Ursula, we're just teasing.

CAITLIN. Aww, Emilio, are we being too mean to you – ?

EMILIO *emerges from the house just as* CAITLIN *is shouting and fake-shoots her in the face.*

EMILIO. POW! / Shut the fuck up.

FRANCISCO *startles a bit.* KRISTINA *notices.*

FRANCISCO. Whoa.

Beat, then –

(Laughing.) I totally forgot about that until just now! Holy shit!

CAITLIN. Ursula started it earlier.

KRISTINA. I always thought it was stupid.

EMILIO. No, you didn't.

KRISTINA. Yes, I did. You didn't even want to start saying anything, because you didn't know if you'd make it through your story without someone sticking a fake grenade in your mouth.

URSULA. Who actually did that?

KRISTINA. Simon did.

EMILIO. Here. This is Alena.

Everyone gathers around, as he clicks through, and coos.

KRISTINA. Oh, wow. She looks literally just like you.

FRANCISCO. Totally. She's beautiful, bro.

KRISTINA. Is this her mother?

EMILIO. Yes...

KRISTINA. She's surprisingly pretty...

EMILIO *takes a drink and immediately spits his back out and hops up and down, fanning his mouth.*

EMILIO. AHHHHHHHHHHHHHHHHHHHHHH!

Everyone except CAITLIN *sort of bursts out laughing.*

KRISTINA. Oh God! I forgot we did that! I forgot we did that!

EMILIO. AH WHAT THE FUCK YOU GUYS AH!!!

FRANCISCO. Hold on, buddy! Hold on! I'll get you some water!

EMILIO *(kind of crying, high, running inside)*. WHAT THE FAAAAAAAAAAAAAAAHHHH –

CAITLIN. What did you guys do?

FRANCISCO. We put a bunch of spicy shit in his drink earlier.

EMILIO. AHHHHHHHHHHHHHHHHHHHHHH!

URSULA....Oh my God. You guys, we're being so mean to Emilio. He's going to kill us.

FRANCISCO. Maybe.

EMILIO. YOU GUYS ARE FUCKING AWFUL WHAT WAS THAT?

URSULA. A bunch of hot sauces.

EMILIO. What the fuck, Ursula?

URSULA. It wasn't my idea! They did it.

EMILIO (*really angry*). What the fuck my tongue is on fire right now! I'm gonna throw up, you fucks!

FRANCISCO (*taking EMILIO by the shoulders*). Hey, E, calm down it was just a joke. It was a prank!

EMILIO. Get the fuck off me!

FRANCISCO. Hey, chill.

EMILIO. No, you chill. Don't fucking put your hands on me. It wasn't fucking funny! I'm gonna puke!

CAITLIN. Emilio, relax…

EMILIO. No, Caitlin! Did someone fucking try to burn off your tastebuds while you were fucking high?

FRANCISCO. You guys are high?

EMILIO. / Yes.

CAITLIN. No.

EMILIO. Caitlin, what? Yes you are?

CAITLIN. No I'm not.

EMILIO. What? You just told me you were 'too stoned for this' like ten minutes ago.

CAITLIN. Yeah, now I'm not anymore.

EMILIO. Caitlin, you are suddenly, for some reason, pretending to not be high because a non-high person just asked you if you were high? That is high-person behavior!

KRISTINA. You two have been stoned this entire time?

EMILIO. No one is actually stoned but Caitlin –

CAITLIN. And Ursula, too! Ursula gave it to us!

Everyone looks at URSULA, *who isn't acting that high.*

URSULA. What? It's legal.

CAITLIN. Don't judge me!

KRISTINA. Who is judging you?

CAITLIN. You are! I can tell!

FRANCISCO. Alright, alright. You know what!? Everybody, let's
    just reel it in. Look, E. I didn't know you were flying high on
    that wacky tobaccy. I'm sorry. I thought we just had a little
    prank war going, alright? You moon us, we spice you. But I'm
    sorry. Let's call a truce and then we can get back to being
    adults adulting, alright?

He holds his hand out to EMILIO, *who doesn't take it.*

Come on. It was a joke.

EMILIO *turns into* DEATH.

DEATH. You know, Emilio is maybe the person here with whom
    I am the least familiar, though we had our run-ins when he was
    a small child – grandparents, childhood pets, et cetera. He is
    among that fortunate class about whom it is said 'their parents
    are still with us,' so even the more routine forms of grief have
    yet to reach him. But, though he may not like to recall it, he
    and I also did have a close call many years ago. A period of
    severe melancholy which activated a tendency towards self-
    destructiveness, not unfamiliar to these creative types.
    Especially when they're young. Substances were involved.

    The formation of a self is... notoriously difficult. And it
    doesn't help if it is being formed in a context in which
    everything about that self feels anathema to said context. The
    gentle bullying of the only environment you know, the only
    history you know – the burden of it. It's easy to feel like an
    aberration. Something to be erased – so why don't you do the
    erasing? The youthful illogic of an incomplete brain. The
    work I do is often thought of as a solution to something, which
    is just not true. In fact, if there's anyone here is considering
    this path – or even feels the desire to consider it – I beg you,

selfishly, to please reconsider. It accounts for the overwhelming majority of anger and regret I find myself managing and I'd really rather not. That is the worst part of the job. Most people, if they can figure out how to wait out the impulse, are fine. Just try and wait it out... Which isn't to say that I'm through with you. Or that things don't just... happen...

EMILIO *becomes* EMILIO *again.*

FRANCISCO. Really, bro, you're not going to shake my hand?

EMILIO. Oh, sorry. I didn't know that's what you were waiting for.

EMILIO *takes* FRANCISCO's *hand and shakes it, but he is looking at* CAITLIN.

FRANCISCO. Is everything good?

EMILIO. Everything's great, 'bro.'

He locks eyes with KRISTINA.

M.E.R.G.E.!

KRISTINA (*redirecting*). Come sit down, Emilio. Simon was saying you have some big art thing happening?

EMILIO. It's not that big...

URSULA. He's actually in this thing called a biennial, which is like this big show of all the big up-and-coming artists from all over the world being big.

KRISTINA. That sounds impressive?

FRANCISCO. That is so cool! I love art.

KRISTINA. Is it photography?

EMILIO. No. I don't take photos anymore.

KRISTINA. What?! No! But you were so good at it! Your wedding photos were the best part of my wedding.

EMILIO. Those might be the last photos I ever took.

KRISTINA. Really? Does that mean they're worth money?

FRANCISCO. You stopped taking photos? But that was like your thing, bro! I feel like Emilio was always running around with a little camera around his neck. Do you guys remember?

KRISTINA. And your locker – remember that? The inside of it was always covered in all those freaky pictures you would, like, rotate in and out from time to time.

URSULA. Like a little exhibit!

KRISTINA. The rest of us just had photos of like Backstreet Boys – but you had all this weird shit. Like that crazy lady who dressed herself up in fat suits and put on all that make-up.

EMILIO. That would be Cindy Sherman. / She's very famous.

KRISTINA. Oh, God. And those kids from Columbine or wherever. That was a whole thing.

CAITLIN. Don't. Emilio just had a whole Columbine moment before you guys got here.

FRANCISCO. Wait. What kids from Columbine?

KRISTINA. There were all these pictures of kids crying after Columbine – or maybe while it was happening? Gathered outside, crying?

URSULA. Oh, right I remember these. Was I with you when you first saw them? We were on some field trip for Honors Journalism to this… news museum? / The Newseum?

KRISTINA. The Newseum.

URSULA. Yes! And there was this exhibit on, like, photos that won some prize…

EMILIO. The Pulitzer / Prize –

URSULA. Right. And it went through all the years. And there were like all those famous photos and I guess the year before was Columbine. It was like picture after picture after picture of teenagers crying and hugging each other. And I remember you were obsessed…

EMILIO. I was. They were beautiful.

KRISTINA. It was very weird. They were in your locker for a long time.

FRANCISCO. So what do you do now if you're not taking photos?

EMILIO. Sound art… installation… sculpture. Can we talk about something else?

KRISTINA. Sound art installation sculpture? What is that?

URSULA. He like, builds these swimming pools and fills them with music and weird sounds, right?

EMILIO (*a little taken aback*). That's… something I have done, yes… How did you know about that?

URSULA. Google.

CAITLIN. Wait, I'm confused. How do you fill a swimming pool with music and weird sounds?

URSULA. They have like… speakers in them? And he fills them with water and the speakers play things that you can only hear if you're actually in the pool, in the water? Like these children's voices speaking in gibberish?

EMILIO. They're saying nursery rhymes.

CAITLIN. That sounds incredibly creepy.

URSULA. But the thing in the biennial is something different, right? Like one of your soundscapes?

EMILIO. Can we please talk about something else?

KRISTINA. No, this is very interesting to me. What is a soundscape?

URSULA. It's like a landscape but with sound? I think it's like a long room with speakers hidden in the walls that are arranged in a certain way playing different sounds? And somehow the vibrations will intersect in different places and take on an almost… physical quality? And you sort of walk through it and somehow people in certain age groups will start to segregate themselves and gather in certain parts of the room based on the sounds they're hearing or something?

CAITLIN. How does that work?

URSULA. I don't know. How does it work, Emilio?

EMILIO. Hey, guess what? I'm done talking about this.

KRISTINA. Why? It sounds interesting.

FRANCISCO. Yeah, now I want to come up and see it.

EMILIO. Please don't.

KRISTINA. Why is this making you so uncomfortable?

EMILIO. I'm not uncomfortable. It's just the last thing I want to talk about right now is my work.

CAITLIN (*loaded*). Why? Because we wouldn't 'get it'?

EMILIO. No? Because it's dumb.

CAITLIN. Because it's dumb… or because we're dumb?

EMILIO. No, Caitlin, because you're dumb. That's the reason I don't want anyone to go because you, specifically, are so dumb that it's just dumbing up the whole place.

URSULA *goes over and cracks* EMILIO*'s neck.*

URSULA. KRRK!

There is a pause, then FRANCISCO *and* KRISTINA *laugh.*

KRISTINA. Oh my God!

FRANCISCO. Ahhh, Ursula!

CAITLIN. Thank you, Ur –

Suddenly, URSULA *cracks* CAITLIN*'s neck.*

URSULA. KRRRK! Stop being so weird, you two!

Another pause, then KRISTINA *and* FRANCISCO *laugh more.* CAITLIN *starts to crack up.*

KRISTINA. / AHHHH!

FRANCISCO. Ohh-ho-ho-hooooo!

CAITLIN. Hey, Ursula!

URSULA, *still giggling and preening, turns around on* CAITLIN, *who in turn, cracks her neck.* URSULA *thinks this is really funny, so she cracks* CAITLIN*'s neck again, then* EMILIO *cracks her neck, and then* CAITLIN*'s neck, and then they're all grabbing at each other's necks trying to fake-crack them. They are high.* KRISTINA, *laughing at first, begins to record it on her phone but she and* FRANCISCO *continue to look on with less and less enthusiasm, and they're realizing they're not high and thus not exactly privy to the enjoyment of the joke. At some point the actual fake-neck-cracking movement gets a little more detailed and the mass sort of begins to form a kind of weird orgy of movement, everyone feeling on each other, everyone's fingers in everyone's hair. At some point,* EMILIO *gets* URSULA *into some sort of sleeper-hold thing, where her back is to him, and his arms are around her head, and he's just cracking her neck over and over and again and she's flailing her arms and can't quite seem to grab him and so she makes a fake gun instead and starts shooting him.*

URSULA. CH-BOOM!

EMILIO. Ahhh, guns!

EMILIO *makes guns, too, starts shooting them. He shoots one at* CAITLIN. KRISTINA *starts getting nervous.*

CAITLIN. CH-CH-BOOM!

EMILIO. CH-BOOM!

KRISTINA. You guys –

KRISTINA *crosses over to break it up.* FRANCISCO *sort of stands there oblivious, drinking his non-drink.* KRISTINA *breaks it up, pretty forcefully.*

You guys, stop. You guys, stop! No guns!

EMILIO. What? Why?

Beat, as KRISTINA *tries to communicate with her eyes. Everyone winds up looking at* FRANCISCO.

FRANCISCO. Yeah, Kristina, why?

Beat. KRISTINA *looks at* FRANCISCO, *who is getting a little incensed.*

KRISTINA. Paco…

Beat.

FRANCISCO. Why shouldn't we pretend to shoot guns? Why is that, Kristina?

KRISTINA. Okay, chill out.

FRANCISCO. Why, Kristina? What's wrong with guns?

KRISTINA. Paco, you know why.

Beat, in which FRANCISCO *suddenly begins to twitch.*

(*Annoyed.*) Paco… This is not –

FRANCISCO *crushes his cup in his hand and begins running around the porch, screaming, crying. Everyone – except* KRISTINA *– gets very quiet and presses themselves against the house or clings to each other. Eventually, he runs off the porch and away into the night, screaming. Beat, before* FRANCISCO *comes running on from the other side of the house, still screaming. He jumps back on to the porch and runs inside the house, the door slamming behind him.*

He's just kidding, you guys. He did this to my parents last night. Excuse me one second.

(*Shouting inside.*) Paco! You cannot just do that to people! It's not funny!

KRISTINA *storms inside after him. Screaming is heard.*

EMILIO. What… the fuck was that!? Ursula, do you know what the fuck is going on?

URSULA. No…

EMILIO. What is going on? Is he sick?

CAITLIN. I mean, it was all about the guns and – maybe it's some sort of PTSD thing –

EMILIO. Whoa, what? Wait. What was he saying about meds earlier?

URSULA. I thought they were for dental work.

EMILIO. Do I feel safe right now? Do you all feel safe? Should we ask him to leave?

The door suddenly opens and FRANCISCO *reappears as if nothing happened, incredibly calm, carrying a speaker.* KRISTINA *comes running after them.*

KRISTINA. I wouldn't have even said anything unless you'd made me!

FRANCISCO. Mind if I borrow this, Ursula?

URSULA. Uh, yes.

KRISTINA. And the last thing I need is you getting triggered on this porch right now and ruining everyone's night, okay?

FRANCISCO. Hey, Berlin, let me borrow your phone? All I've got is a flip phone and I got a feeling you've got better music taste than that one.

EMILIO. Uh, okay –

FRANCISCO. Can you unlock it? What do you use? Spotify?

EMILIO unlocks the phone with a nod and hands it over.

KRISTINA. So you're just going to ignore me?

FRANCISCO. I am, because you're being a bitch.

KRISTINA snatches the phone out of FRANCISCO*'s hand.*

EMILIO. / Whoa –

KRISTINA. Paco, these are our friends!

FRANCISCO. Kristina, / give me the phone back –

KRISTINA. Why is it a problem if I tell them you're sick!?

FRANCISCO. Because I asked you not to!

KRISTINA. But this is different!

FRANCISCO. Kristina, give me the phone back –

EMILIO takes the phone away from KRISTINA.

EMILIO. Actually how about you give me my phone back?

CAITLIN. Paco, are you okay?

Beat. FRANCISCO *looks at* KRISTINA.

FRANCISCO. You heard Kristina. I'm a big sick idiot, right?

KRISTINA. I didn't say you were an idiot – we just don't know your triggers –

FRANCISCO. Well, I can tell you what they're not!

CAITLIN. Paco is it… post-traumatic / stress –

FRANCISCO. No, it's not –

KRISTINA. / Yes –

FRANCISCO. No, it's not, Kristina –

KRISTINA. It was, but then he didn't take care of it so now it's become other things – and all I'm asking him to do is take care now –

EMILIO. / What kinds of things?

FRANCISCO. Right, and so now I'm on like nine thousand fucking pills, which Kristina knows all about –

KRISTINA. / It's not 'nine thousand pills' –

FRANCISCO. – and yet she thinks I'm such a fucking baby that I can't take the sight of a bunch of assholes playing fake guns – even though she's supposed to be a fucking doctor. Isn't that right, Kristina? I'm not a basket case! This isn't a movie! I'm not about to hallucinate a battlefield! I'm fine, everybody! I'm on medication, I'm not drinking, and it's fine! Everybody happy?

Beat, in which KRISTINA *seems sheepish.* FRANCISCO *slips the phone out of* EMILIO*'s hand.*

Now listen. I'm sensing there's a lot of weird tension on this porch and so I'm about to subject you all to a very classic method of military discipline called Sweating Out the Bullshit, because this is not the night to let a few too many puffs on the magic dragon yuck the collective yum, mmkay? This is the St Anthony's Class of 2002 twentieth reunion M.E.R.G.E. pre-reunion… reunion and we're not going anywhere until we reset this mothertrucking vibe. So I suggest you sluts get ready to work.

FRANCISCO *taps his phone and something dance-y and early-oughties begins to play.* FRANCISCO *jumps up and starts to dance.*

KRISTINA. Francisco –

FRANCISCO. Shut up.

He grabs EMILIO *and shoves him into her.*

Emilio, dance with my cousin. Everybody has to dance!

FRANCISCO *turns the music up. Everyone gradually, awkwardly, starts dancing until it actually sort of begins to turn into something fun.* FRANCISCO *goes up to* URSULA *and dances with her.* FRANCISCO *goes up to* CAITLIN *and starts dancing with her.* FRANCISCO *sort of dances with* URSULA *and* CAITLIN, *but* CAITLIN *is clearly only dancing with* FRANCISCO. CAITLIN *kind of closes her eyes, whips her hair around.* FRANCISCO *is into it.* EMILIO *watches, while* KRISTINA *just pours herself another drink while talking to him, but we have no idea what they're saying. Meanwhile,* FRANCISCO *becomes* DEATH.

DEATH. And then there are certain individuals, like Paco, who are more than known to me. In fact, they are something more like familiars. They have not only borne witness to some of my more complicated… assignments… but, at times, may have even been agents in my endeavors. This familiarity, however, does come with a cost. There is a point at which we can become so… intimate, there is no turning back. A life is not a thing you can untake. And it's hard enough to unremember one death, let alone several, let alone… a massacre. In general, I do try and go about my business with some degree of surreptitiousness, but multiple exposures to my handiwork does tend to reveal my patterns. You begin to see me everywhere. You become the eyes I have the hardest time hiding from, which can be a little uncomfortable for me. In fact, Francisco's been watching me ever since he showed up here – or perhaps the word is 'felt?' But actually he feels me everywhere constantly. I suspect he feels me moving around inside him at this very moment… Of course, that sort of sensitivity, unchecked, takes its toll. So one must find ways to distract oneself. You get very good at distractions, trying uselessly to get back to the state of blind blissfulness that everyone else seems to enjoy. So, sure, he's 'fine.' Whatever 'fine' means... Hey, are you familiar with this notion of the *Danse Macabre*?

FRANCISCO *becomes* FRANCISCO. *Everyone dances until* CAITLIN *sees someone offstage, on another porch, who seems to be trying to get someone's attention. She taps* URSULA *on the shoulder.* CAITLIN *points.*

CAITLIN (*chanting*). There's a lady! There's a lady!

EVERYONE. Hey, lady! Hey, lady! Hey, lady!

URSULA *sees the neighbor, is mouthing, 'Sorry! Sorry!' She crosses to the speakers and turns down the music. Everyone has noticed and stopped dancing.*

URSULA. Sorry! I'm so sorry!

The neighbor goes back inside.

Sorry, guys. I think we have to keep it down. I forgot about my neighbors.

FRANCISCO. It's not even eight o'clock! The sun isn't even completely down.

URSULA. I know, but she's old.

FRANCISCO. Should I go talk to her? I can talk to her! Old ladies love me –

URSULA. No. We can dance but we just have to keep the music down...

FRANCISCO (*looking through the phone*). I can find something chiller...

KRISTINA *is on her phone, calling* SIMON. *He doesn't pick up.*

KRISTINA (*leaving a message*). Hi Simon's voicemail. Do you hear that? We're having a great time...

She holds the phone up to the music, then –

(*Screams into the phone.*) How dare you!?

Hangs up, then her phone dings.

Oh, you guys! The limo has been dispatched! Our driver's name is Miguel. That's a sexy name. Come get me, Miguel. Damn these are really hitting, Ursula. ETA is... twenty-five minutes!? No! We're already late, Miguel. What the fuck, Miguel?

EMILIO *catches* CAITLIN'*s eye over* FRANCISCO'*s shoulder. They make faces at each other.* EMILIO *is like 'What are you doing?'* CAITLIN *rolls her eyes.*

URSULA....Does anyone else need another drink before you go?

CAITLIN. I'll have one more. But just like half of one.

KRISTINA. Actually, let me get another double.

EMILIO *attempts to take the drink out of* KRISTINA'*s hand.*

EMILIO. Okay, maybe it's time to cut you off –

KRISTINA *snatches it away.*

KRISTINA. You know, you're getting a little too into snatching things out of my hands. Are you trying to die tonight?!

EMILIO. Kristina, I feel like maybe you should slow down with the jungle juice.

KRISTINA. I don't need you to tell me to slow down. In fact, how about you catch up?

EMILIO. Kristina –

KRISTINA (*drunk*). No, Emilio! Why are you always trying to be the boss of everybody? I would have thought that you would have outgrown this shit. No one died and made you CEO of everything, CEO of the Multiculti Reject Club, or whatever. It's bullshit. So, you know what? There's no CEO here. There's only the doctor! And the doctor's orders are that you drink! Here!

She pours him a drink, then everyone.

In fact, let me pour everyone a drink because this is the first night I've had to myself in like a million years and I am not about to waste it on a bunch of Deborah Downers downing around all over my downtown. We're supposed to be feeling good! This is supposed to be a good time – This one is for you, Mr Plant –

They stop her from pouring jungle juice into one of the planters.

EMILIO. Kristina… are you blacked out?

Beat, before KRISTINA *calmly sets the cup and pitcher of jungle juice down.*

KRISTINA. Emilio, I am a fucking anesthesiologist with a subspecialty in twilight fucking therapies. Do you know that means? That means I literally give people ante-fucking-rograde fucking amnesias on the daily so I think I would know if I was blacked the fuck out, but thank you very much.

(*Turning on* CAITLIN.) And, Caitlin, I would really appreciate it if you would stop going around town telling everybody about the one time I maybe 'browned out' with you after a thirty-hour shift, okay? I was tired!

CAITLIN. It was more than once.

KRISTINA. / It's not more than once!

CAITLIN. And I am concerned for you. I'm your friend!

KRISTINA. Oh okay, well you can be a better friend and be more concerned about yourself! I'm certainly not going around to everyone talking about how much you resent your stepkids after two spicy margaritas or start to fantasize about walking out on your old-man husband!

CAITLIN. Whoa, excuse me –

KRISTINA. You're excused! You don't know what it's like! None of you! I get one night in a blue moon to myself like this – one night! Meanwhile, I am the only person in my family holding every fucking thing together. Plus my cousin just got back from God Knows Where doing God Knows What except living on the streets and scaring the fuck out of his family and now he hates me even though I'm the only person competent enough to manage everything because my parents are getting so old and all my grown adult husband wants to do all day is play video games! And I have so… many kids, you guys! I have so many… fucking kids! I spent my entire twenties either pregnant or in med school!

She starts crying. Beat.

So I'm not fucking blacked out, okay? I'm just… alone!

KRISTINA *runs inside, upset.* URSULA *hurries after her.*

URSULA. Kristina…?

EMILIO, CAITLIN, *and* FRANCISCO *look at each other.*

EMILIO. Should we go in?

FRANCISCO. Nah. She'll be fine. She has to drink like this so she can get her feelings out.

FRANCISCO *pulls* CAITLIN *in and they start to dance.*

CAITLIN. But I feel bad.

FRANCISCO. Kristina's gonna be fine. I want to keep dancing.

He notices EMILIO *watching them, flicking his tongue in the air.*

You want in on this?

Fed up, EMILIO *just goes inside.* CAITLIN *and* FRANCISCO *keep dancing.*

What's going on between you two?

CAITLIN. Nothing. He's just European. I don't know.

FRANCISCO. I'm not gonna blame that on Europe. I always remembered he was kind of like this. Like he's always had a… pissy constitution.

CAITLIN (*laughs*). Yeah. A little bit… When did you become such a dancer?

FRANCISCO. Believe it or not, you do a lot of dancing in the Marines.

CAITLIN. Really? Who do you dance with?

FRANCISCO. Uh. Each other. You ever YouTubed 'Marines dance party in Iraq?'

CAITLIN. No.

FRANCISCO. Okay, well please don't. I may have gone viral in a way I did not intend and I'd like to maintain whatever shreds of respect you might still have for me.

CAITLIN. Paco, what are you talking about?! I have so much respect for you.

FRANCISCO. Really? That means a lot.

Beat.

CAITLIN. Why did Kristina say you were living on the streets?

Beat.

FRANCISCO. She's exaggerating a little bit. She doesn't understand. I couldn't afford to pay my rent for a bit so I just thought, why don't I get a little bit lost, for a little while. That's all. I knew how to survive in the desert. That's all LA was. Another desert... It wasn't as bad as she's making it seem. It was like... an extended hike. Like camping. But it is why I stopped writing. I would think all the time, 'I should reach out.' But days just keep stacking up, man, and you look up and... But I still have your messages. Every single one. Those messages really meant a lot to me, you know. You'll never know how much they meant to me. Even though, I wasn't writing, I still read them. I read them, every day, all of them. Whenever I could get to a computer. They got me through what happened to me in Fallujah. They got me through again – through the other desert. I feel like I only came here, so I could look you in the eye and say thank you. You saved my life.

CAITLIN. I couldn't have been the only person writing to you.

FRANCISCO. True. But your messages were the only ones I could be bothered with. Everyone else's were so... I don't know. Nothing? Just updates on what people were doing. Daddy just retired, Kristina just finished her rotation. Everything was all about the present for them, their present but, you know, when you're out there, you start to feel... outside of it. You start to live on your own timeline. Everything seems to be happening to everyone else somewhere else. And you were the only person who would talk to me about the shit I knew about – the things I could remember. You kept me reminded of who I really was – all these little stories it felt like you were keeping for me... Like that time we drove to the school football field after-hours and messed around under the bleachers. Remember that? We almost got caught by that poor night janitor, that Haitian guy? He dropped to his knees and started praying. I guess he thought we were ghosts. A pair of ghosts under the bleachers. Man, I almost felt bad. You said you thought about it anytime you heard anyone talking French and now the same thing happens to me... But that was a good story... I can't believe I'd almost lost it.

Beat.

Anyway, I should have reached out, but, uh, I didn't think you'd want to be bothered with all that. It was... you know. But it's behind me now! I'm here. I'm back. Whatever that's going to mean.

Beat.

How's your family?

CAITLIN. Oh, they're great. Brock's starting law school. Olivia's in college.

FRANCISCO (*whistles*). Wow. That's crazy.

CAITLIN. What's crazy is they're basically the age I was when I married their father and I just think, you know, like... Man...

FRANCISCO....Man?

CAITLIN. I don't know. I look at them and can't help but look back on myself at that age and I just think I didn't know... anything. I didn't know how much time I really had ahead of me. I thought I was at the end of something. I thought I had to hurry up before... some sort of door closed. I look at them and almost feel... jealous? They have like a whole life ahead of them. I just didn't feel that way. I didn't feel like I had a whole life ahead of me.

FRANCISCO. Are you... unhappy?

CAITLIN. No, I'm happy! Of course!

FRANCISCO. / Oh, yeah! Yeah!

CAITLIN. I'm happy! I love them. I love my family. Michael's... a lot. He needs to stay off the internet but he's a good provider. I've made peace with... uh, myself. You just... say things sometimes. You know how it is.

FRANCISCO. I thought so. You seem happy... If anyone's jealous, it's me. Michael hit the jackpot.

Beat.

I wish I'd figured out how to have a family – have kids. Sometimes I think that would've, uh, made all the difference.

CAITLIN. You can... still have kids.

FRANCISCO. Uh, we'll see about that. We'll see if anybody still wants this... whatever this is, this mess... I wish we had figured ourselves out. You think we could have ever had kids?

Beat.

CAITLIN. Probably.

FRANCISCO. I guess it's too late now. That's the straw I drew, huh?

Beat.

CAITLIN. I'm going to kiss you.

FRANCISCO. You are?

CAITLIN. Yeah. For old times' sake. I want to remember what it's like. Let's do it.

They kiss. EMILIO *is at the door.*

EMILIO. Paco, I really think you should go see Kristina.

FRANCISCO. Why?

EMILIO. She's crying uncontrollably and begging for you... specifically.

FRANCISCO. Jesus.

(*To* CAITLIN.) Don't move! This dance isn't over!

FRANCISCO *goes inside with a clip in his step. Something about the old him has returned.* EMILIO *and* CAITLIN *are alone. At some point, the music changes into something kind of unmelodic and arrhythmic and weird and annoying.*

EMILIO. What do you think you're doing?!

CAITLIN. We're just dancing. Will you get out of my face?

EMILIO. That was not fucking dancing, Caitlin. And you know it wasn't.

CAITLIN. What are you? My dad?

EMILIO. God forbid, because then you might marry me and then cheat on me with your high-school boyfriend… I think you need to recognize that you're not in your right mind. Is this not familiar to you?

CAITLIN. What are you even talking about?

EMILIO. This is how he always used to come to you. I thought this was always how he did it, when you were… drunk, when you were –

CAITLIN. Emilio, you have no idea what you're talking about, so please shut up.

EMILIO. You know what? You're right. You're an adult. Ruin your own life if you want to.

CAITLIN. Ruin my life?

EMILIO. Yeah, your cushy little suburban life babysitting your retired cop who you / apparently hate?

CAITLIN. You are actually getting on my nerves.

EMILIO. You weren't able to stop yourself back then. Why should it be any different now?

Beat.

Did this man coerce you or were you not coerced?… Did he force you or didn't he?

CAITLIN. Why are you bringing shit up from a thousand years ago!?

EMILIO. Because I need to understand what's real and what's not real. I need to decide if I wasted my life or not, believing you weren't a fucking first-class sociopath.

CAITLIN *fake breaks his neck.*

CAITLIN. KRK! I said, stop it!

EMILIO. Does that man even know what he did to you?

CAITLIN. You don't know anything. You were not there –

EMILIO. I was there for the aftermath, Caitlin. / I was there every fucking time –

CAITLIN. You don't know what you're talking about so shut – the fuck – up.

KRISTINA, URSULA, *and* FRANCISCO *appear at the door.* KRISTINA *is a messy drunk.*

KRISTINA. But I feel like you hate me, Paco.

FRANCISCO. I don't hate you, Kristina. You just need some fresh air.

KRISTINA. I just wanted you to have a fun time tonight…

FRANCISCO. I am having a fun time…

KRISTINA *sees* CAITLIN *and* EMILIO *together.*

KRISTINA. Ugh! Will you two just make out already?

The music is at its most annoying.

UGH! WHAT THE FUCK IS THIS NOISE! THIS IS LIKE HELL! MAKE IT STOP!

KRISTINA *just starts kind of kicking at the speaker like some sort of animal, which* EMILIO *rushes over to stop.*

EMILIO. Whoa! Whoa! Whoa! Kristina! That's not yours!

KRISTINA. Whoops, sorry. I'm sorry, Emilio. I'm sorry, everyone. I don't know… I don't know what I'm doing…

EMILIO. It's okay…

KRISTINA (*messy, touching him*). I'm so sorry… I'm so sorry…

EMILIO. Kristina, it's fine…

KRISTINA. I'm so sorry I led people to believe you were gay. That wasn't right of me. I just… I don't know. Maybe I'm homophobic because I sometimes think I might be gay but

I don't know. I don't know if I'm actually gay or if I just want
a divorce. And I think I also don't know if I want to be
a doctor anymore but I don't know how to do anything else.
Also my cousin hates me. Everyone hates me.

FRANCISCO. No one hates you but let's have some more water?

KRISTINA. Okay.

Beat.

CAITLIN. Kristina, do you want to talk?

KRISTINA. About what?

EMILIO. About any of the five million things you just brought
up?

KRISTINA. Oh, right… Um…

Sighs.

I just feel like… I'm an amazing Catholic, you know? I did
everything the Church told me to do. I had a whole army of
Baby Catholics. I honored my parents and my grandparents.
I devoted my life to service – not just to the sick but to my
actual country. I thought I was supposed feel more and more
sure, right? More and more clear about my life, my purpose,
and all I feel is… dimmer and lost and stupid and tired all the
time. I don't feel any closer to God. I don't even feel that
close to myself. And then there's this colleague at work,
Cassandra. She's a neurosurgeon and she's a lesbian and she's
so beautiful – she has this really incredible skin and these soft-
looking lips and her voice – I just really love the sound of her
voice. It's very warm and calming and sounds the way velvet
feels. We started working together during COVID, when every
surgeon in the hospital was like all hands on deck and it really
feels like we really trauma bonded and now she sort of taps
me for whatever she can because she prefers working with
other female doctors of color and I just think that's so rad and
I always look forward to surgeries with her because she's also
just so fucking good at her job – which is not an easy job, you
know? Like removing people's tumors while they're still
awake and shit. She's so good, she makes me want to do
a better job, you know. She'll do this thing where I'll look

over at her on like hour two of stopping a brain bleed or
something and she'll just, like, wink at me? And I know it's
like a half-joke but it's actually just what I need, you know? It
gives me a little extra boost to keep going, because this job is
so stressful and the stakes are so high, like keeping people on
the other side of dying. She's so consistent and so grounded
and so competent. And sometimes I find myself thinking, 'Is
this because she's a lesbian?' Or something? Like what is it
about her life that allows her to, like, exude all this...
amazingness? Is she, somehow, freer than me? And then I find
myself comparing her and Cameron, like all the time. Sort of
without my even thinking about it. But it's not like I feel that
about anyone else but Cassandra. It's just her. So I don't know.
It's just. It's so confused.

Beat.

FRANCISCO. You can be a lesbian, Kristina, it's okay.

KRISTINA. That's not the point, Paco! I'm just lost. I don't
know what happened to me. I feel so far away from... what
I understood about myself. It's like I don't remember why
I made the choices I did or how. And I don't know how
a pandemic can do that... I feel like... I feel like I died, which
is an insane thing to say because I quite literally had entire
rooms full of people die on me, so many colleagues. I mean,
we had refrigerator trucks outside our hospital for weeks
because there wasn't room enough... But I feel like now I'm
in this afterlife and before, there was the beforelife. And now
I don't quite know... I can't quite figure out how to make
them both work in my head. I can't quite figure out what one
has to do with the other and I worry if I can't figure this out,
I'll go crazy...

Beat.

URSULA. Do you want some pot?

Everyone gestures to URSULA *like, 'No, no, no!'*

KRISTINA. No, Ursula. But that's very sweet of you. I just want
my limo! Sometimes I think high school was the last time
I really liked myself, that I knew what I was doing. I want to
remind myself of what that was like – what it was like to feel

smart and talented and full of promise and good at things and like I had a bunch of amazing friends! And, Ursula, you are coming with me!

URSULA. No, I'm not.

KRISTINA. Come on, Ursula! Please! You have to! Simon already cancelled! What do you think is going to happen? What's the worst thing that could happen?

Beat, as URSULA *stands and begins to gather various empty cups and bowls.*

URSULA. Okay, listen: I really appreciate everyone's commitment to my coming out but I am starting to feel a little offended and I'd like you all to stop. I'm not entirely sure where this is coming from – I don't know if it's guilt, I don't know if it's pity – but rest assured that you didn't do this to me and you can't undo it and going to this reunion is not actually going to make me feel any better. I've been to many reunions before this. I know what happens. And I already have a hard enough time getting around crowds in daylight. I don't know what the lighting situation is going be like there. So I'd rather not put up with any unnecessary discomfort. What's fun for you may not necessarily be fun for me anymore and that's alright. I'm so happy to just be here, doing this. I don't need anything else from my night. So just leave it alone, okay?

EMILIO. Okay…

Beat.

KRISTINA *(a tantrum)*. No! Come on, Ursula! Come on, please! I don't accept that.

URSULA. Kristina, the answer is no!

FRANCISCO. Come on, Kristina. Relax.

URSULA *exits inside to put things away.*

EMILIO *(to FRANCISCO)*. Paco, I'm just curious…

FRANCISCO. Uh-huh…

EMILIO. What did you and Caitlin even talk about? When you guys started chatting again?

FRANCISCO *and* CAITLIN *share a look.*

FRANCISCO (*laughs*). Ha ha ha ha. All kinds of stuff.

EMILIO. Did you guys ever talk about the break-up?

FRANCISCO. Ha ha ha, I mean a little bit, you know?

EMILIO. Oh, really? Wait it was Caitlin who called it off, right?

FRANCISCO. Yeah.

CAITLIN. Why are we talking about this?

EMILIO. Because I want to remember, Caitlin! Why did you break up again? I don't remember.

FRANCISCO. Well, I mean, we were young, you know. I was older. We were in different phases of our lives. I get it. She was going to college. I wasn't going to college.

EMILIO. Was that really why?

FRANCISCO. Do you think there was another reason?

EMILIO. There wasn't like a thing that happened?

FRANCISCO. What kind of thing?

URSULA *re-enters.*

EMILIO. Ursula, do you remember why Paco and Caitlin broke up?

URSULA (*leery*). I do not...

EMILIO. Kristina?

KRISTINA. What the hell are we even talking about?

EMILIO. Caitlin, wasn't there a reason?

CAITLIN. Emilio, there was no reason. What is wrong with you?

EMILIO. Wasn't Kristina just talking about going back? I want to go back too, and retrace my steps.

(*Pointed.*) I don't wanna keep walking around not knowing what I'm talking about. I'm trying to get the facts straight.

KRISTINA*'s phone starts ringing. She looks at it.*

KRISTINA. It's Simon! Simon's calling! Shut up! Shut up!

URSULA. Answer it! Put him on speaker!

KRISTINA (*answers it*). Simon?!

SIMON (*on phone*). Hey!!!

URSULA. Hey, Simon!

SIMON. Oh wow. Hi, Ursula!

KRISTINA. We're pissed at you!

SIMON. Oh noooo! Don't be pissed! I feel so bad!

URSULA. Well, we are. Where are you?!

SIMON. I literally just got out of the office. I just finished filing for today. I'm so sorry I can't be there but AI is about to get wild.

URSULA. Well we miss you.

SIMON. I thought you guys would have left already.

KRISTINA. Um. We were supposed to but we were running late and now the limo's running late. It's a whole thing.

SIMON. Is that Emilio sulking in the corner over there?

EMILIO. Hey, Si.

SIMON. Emilio, WTF dude, I got your texts. I'm so sorry.

EMILIO. It's fine… Hey, Si, quick question: was Paco in M.E.R.G.E.?

SIMON. What? Of course not!

EMILIO. Yeah, that's what I thought. We were all just trying to remember. And do you remember why Caitlin dumped him?

SIMON. Eek. Wasn't it because things got weird?

KRISTINA. What does that mean?

SIMON. Like didn't things start to get a little date-rapey or something? No?

FRANCISCO, *hearing this, stalks over to* EMILIO.

EMILIO. Right, and so would you believe this shit?

FRANCISCO *snatches the phone away from* EMILIO.

FRANCISCO. Hey, Simon.

SIMON. Oh my God!… Hi Paco…

FRANCISCO. Hi, Simon…

SIMON. Are you… back in Maryland?

FRANCISCO. I am.

SIMON. Oh man… It's so good to see you!… Is everything okay?

FRANCISCO. Yeah, everything's totally great. Do you want to say more about date rape, Simon?

SIMON. I mean, maybe I… maybe I was… wrong? I don't… I thought maybe Emilio… listen, I don't know what's going on?

EMILIO. Well, what do you call it, Caitlin?

KRISTINA. What is going on?

EMILIO. What do you call it?

CAITLIN. What do I call what?

FRANCISCO. Did I… do something wrong?

SIMON. Should I call / back?

EMILIO. Did you?

FRANCISCO (*looking at* CAITLIN). Umm…

EMILIO. I heard you 'didn't like the feel of rubber.'

CAITLIN (*angry*). Emilio, stop talking right now…

EMILIO. I heard every time she asked, you would refuse. Is that true?

CAITLIN. Emilio!

EMILIO. Do you know how many times I was driving her to a fucking clinic? Walking her past all those crazies with their posterboards? Holding her hand in those cold waiting rooms? Do you know how many times they mistook me for the one who did it? The looks I got. Why wasn't it ever you, Paco? Why was it you weren't ever there?

(*To* CAITLIN.) Why didn't you ever ask him to come? Was it because you were scared? Did he scare you? Did you scare her, Paco?

CAITLIN. There is something seriously wrong with you.

EMILIO. Wrong with me or wrong with you? The first time, we can call it a mistake. The second time, it's a worry. The third time, it's either a problem or it's a pattern. But if it wasn't him forcing you, Caitlin, why was it so hard for you to get what you wanted?

Beat.

(*To* FRANCISCO.) Why was it so hard for Caitlin to get what she wanted?… Anybody?

FRANCISCO *drops to the ground and starts convulsing.* KRISTINA *sees this, rushes over to her cousin, taking the phone with her.*

KRISTINA. Paco?… Paco! Jesus – someone, pillows please!

URSULA *runs inside.* KRISTINA *is trying to put him on his side, while* CAITLIN *hovers, panicked.* EMILIO *hangs back.*

Move all this shit, if you want to be helpful! So he doesn't hurt himself!

CAITLIN *goes over to hold down his legs.* URSULA *comes back out with pillows. By this point,* FRANCISCO *has likely soiled himself.* EMILIO *finally realizes what's going on, approaches everyone.*

EMILIO. What's happening?

KRISTINA. It's a seizure! Get away!

EMILIO. But –

KRISTINA. PLEASE JUST GET AWAY!

Beat.

You could get hurt.

URSULA. What do we do?

KRISTINA (*looking at her watch*). You can't do anything! You just have to wait for it to stop! If it's longer than five minutes, we have to go to the hospital.

KRISTINA *turns into* DEATH, *with* FRANCISCO *seizing at its feet.*

DEATH. You would think that I would have a sort of love–hate relationship with doctors – that somehow they would get in my way – but I don't really see them like that. I like doctors. I like Kristina. I admire anyone who submits themselves to a higher calling – especially if that calling comes with an ethical code. Those are my favorites. And I actually think there's a lot of overlap here – or synergy – between what they do and what I do, philosophically speaking. Yes, they are supposed to 'save lives,' but what does that really mean? If anything, they extend them, which is fine, because what am I in a rush for? And that extension does tend to make people... wiser, more thoughtful, considerate. And that pleases me.

Yes, what I appreciate about doctors, more than anything, is the work they do in preparing for my interceding. It used to be more people had no idea what was happening and I will tell you that that was exhausting. It used to be a whole lot of 'Wait, what!? What!? What's going on!?' Now it's much more, 'Oh? Okay.' And I like that. I like to see them brave.

Watches FRANCISCO.

I think I may have mentioned earlier – or maybe I didn't? – that I actually am here for work. But when am I never working, am I right? Ha ha ha ha, no, no, um... It's tempting to think that this one here is the reason why, but no, my brief is...

Looks around at the group.

...slightly more complex.

Looks at FRANCISCO.

But this is always an interesting thing to watch... In fact, some of your predecessors once considered this to be the most sacred of states, the complete loss of control, the body's rebellion, that in the throes of this you were peeking somewhat behind the veil, touching the hem of the divine, the mystical. And, in fact, I think he can see me now… Hello, Francisco… Old friend… You're fine… 'Go Cindy! Go Cindy!'

Laughs.

I kid. You're going to be fine.

FRANCISCO *stops seizing, is unconscious.* KRISTINA *becomes* KRISTINA *again.*

KRISTINA. Thank God.

(*Gently nudging him.*) Cisco? Francisco? Paco?

Beat.

CAITLIN. Francisco?

FRANCISCO *sort of comes to.*

FRANCISCO (*confused, tired*). Fuck. What? Ow.

KRISTINA. Paco, you just had a seizure.

FRANCISCO. Fuck.

KRISTINA. You just had a seizure.

FRANCISCO. Fuck me. Did I piss myself? Man.

CAITLIN. Stop it. Don't be embarrassed. It wasn't your fault.

FRANCISCO. Who – Caitlin?

KRISTINA. Just rest.

Beat.

Guys, he's disoriented. He has to regain his bearings.

CAITLIN. Well it looks like you got your wish, Emilio!

KRISTINA. What?

CAITLIN. Earlier, Emilio said he didn't even want Paco to be here.

EMILIO. I did not say that!

CAITLIN. You liar. You were literally standing there going 'Do I feel safe?' When it's actually been you, *you* who we should

have been safe from – with all your negativity, all your
negativity all fucking night, picking at him and picking at all
of us and being so judgmental – all night!

EMILIO. Well, first of all, let me point out that I did not start this
seizure. I'm not the reason this guy is sick. In fact, it sounds
like the war is what fucking started these seizures, correct,
Kristina? And, second of all, let's not sit here and act like my
magnificent powers of judgment are capable of actually
making anyone do anything. I mean, I wish my judgment
actually mattered here or anywhere else, but it doesn't. Why
do you think I fucking got out of this stupid country?

CAITLIN. Oh shut up. See? This is what I'm talking about.

EMILIO. If my judgment actually mattered so much, you
wouldn't be running around trying to relive the worst mistake
you've ever made.

KRISTINA. Please stop talking –

EMILIO. If my judgment fucking mattered, you would have
gotten out of this town and done something with yourself and
not gotten stuck like a sad-sack loser! To be honest, I'd rather
have this judgment than poor judgment. Or no judgment.
Which one of those fucked you up, huh? Top of the class,
every class, every fucking honors class – one of the most
intelligent people I've ever known – and now what? Stuck
with two kids you hate and a bigot for a husband, throwing
yourself at damaged goods. What a waste!

KRISTINA. Hey! / Hey! HEY! EMILIO, STOP! HEY!

EMILIO. Do you think you're going to fix him. Is that what's
going to give your life value again? Newsflash: fucking
somebody is not going to fix them and it's not going to fix you.

KRISTINA. Emilio! I think you need to shut your mouth right
now!

EMILIO. Excuse me.

KRISTINA. Let me remind you that my cousin served five tours
of duty fighting for your rights and your freedoms, so show
some respect –

EMILIO. Let me stop you right there. He didn't fight this war for me. I've been fucking living in the middle of Europe for the past thirteen years. I have fucking citizenship –

KRISTINA. Oh, right, then why don't you take yourself back there, / you ungrateful dick –

EMILIO. And he didn't fight this war – this fucking endless war – he didn't fight it for Caitlin either. Or Ursula. Or you. You weren't fighting for us. You were at work. You were working for a bunch of wealthy douchetards who aren't really so different from the ones I work for! So don't you start calling me ungrateful! Paco is not a fucking saint or a hero. Paco was an employee. I'm sorry he thought he was working for us, but he wasn't. I don't know how I'm supposed to suddenly feel something for an adult who is suffering from his own uninformed adult choices. All I can do is feel sorry for him. That's it. So if you brought him here for us to feel sorry for him, here it is, Kristina!

(*To* FRANCISCO.) Hey, Paco, employee to employee, I feel so sorry for you. I'm sorry that this happened to you. I'm sorry that a bunch of people you will never meet encouraged you to risk your life to fill their pockets. I'm sorry you were tricked and now you have to deal with that damage for the rest of your life. And I'm sorry you were brought up to think that there was some sort of honor in rape and theft and pillage and killing and taking whatever you thought you deserved and I'm sorry it looks like you're finally getting what you actually deserve. I'm sorry. I'm sorry. I'm sorry.

Beat, before the limo is heard pulling up. Everyone watches it pull in.

And here's your fucking limo.

KRISTINA. You know what? Everyone, let's go. Emilio, you can fucking walk to the reunion – no, crawl like the baby you are, for all I care. But you're not getting into that limo with me.

EMILIO. / Oh boo hoo hoo.

KRISTINA. You're not about to ruin my night any more than you already have. And I don't need to see your face ever again. Paco, let's go.

FRANCISCO. I pissed my pants...

KRISTINA. We can stop and get some club soda and hang them out the window to dry.

FRANCISCO. Okay... But what about the thing? I saw the thing.

KRISTINA. Saw what thing?

FRANCISCO. The thing that's here for something, for someone.

KRISTINA and FRANCISCO exit but CAITLIN lingers.

CAITLIN. You know, I actually feel sorry for you.

EMILIO. I actually feel sorry for you.

CAITLIN. No, you feel sorry for someone else. And I feel sorry for her, too, but she's not here right now. She's not here anymore. It's just me.

EMILIO. Prove it.

CAITLIN. Prove what? You're insane.

Beat.

Ursula, are you coming?

URSULA *hesitates.*

CAITLIN. Everyone here's just a sad-sack loser who got stuck, that means you, too.

EMILIO. Leave her out of this.

CAITLIN. Emilio, who are you kidding? All she's done all night is show you how much she cares about you, you and your stupid art, showering you with every kind word under the sun, and what have you done? Besides shut her down. Make her feel stupid – make all of us feel stupid – when actually you're the stuck one.

After a hesitation, URSULA steps off the porch.

EMILIO. Ursula...

She ignores him and exits with CAITLIN, leaving EMILIO alone.

Fuck you! I'll call a fucking car!

The sounds of the car pulling off, as EMILIO *takes out his phone.*

Fucking stupid…

Immediately, his phone begins to buzz. FaceTime.

Jesus Christ.

Answers it.

Hey Simon.

SIMON (*on phone*). Emilio, what the fuck just happened?! Kristina's not picking up!

EMILIO. A bunch of bullshit. Paco had a seizure.

SIMON. What?!

EMILIO. He's fine. He only pissed himself. They're gone.

SIMON. Gone where?

EMILIO. To the reunion.

SIMON. What the fuck!? Was it what I said?

EMILIO. No, no –

SIMON. I mean what did I just call in to? It felt like an ambush.

EMILIO. This whole night's been an ambush. Kristina brought him here as a 'surprise,' but really it was all so we could sit here and play-act like he was actually our friend and not a complete dick all night long. Meanwhile, he and Caitlin were basically fucking each other in front of everyone.

SIMON. What?

EMILIO. Yeah. Yeah, you really missed a party. Maybe if you'd been here I would have felt different. It wouldn't have been so fucking awful.

SIMON. Man… Fuck… okay… God… I mean, Paco was a dick, but I didn't mean to…

EMILIO. Let it go. Fifteen fucking years, man.

SIMON. What happened fifteen years ago?

EMILIO. That was the last time I saw everyone. Kristina's wedding.

SIMON. Oh, right. You took the photos.

EMILIO. Yeah... The last I ever took.

SIMON. Right... God, that was one of the most awkward weddings of my life. Wasn't that when we all met Michael for the first time? It was like hanging out with our dad.

EMILIO. Yeah...

Beat.

SIMON. So are you going to go to the reunion?

EMILIO. Fuck no. I'm going to head back to my hotel, see if the spa's open or something.

SIMON. Man... I forgot you stopped taking photographs. What happened?

EMILIO. Yeah I got tired of mimesis.

SIMON. What?

EMILIO. Never mind.

SIMON. You know what I was thinking about? All those photos you took on 9/11. Do you remember this? When it happened, the principal pulled us all – you, me, Kristina, Caitlin – out of homeroom to, like, monitor the halls, do you remember that? And he was like, 'You guys are the honors students, you're in charge' as if that meant anything...

EMILIO. Yeah.

SIMON. And remember we were walking through those halls together and we didn't know what the fuck to do? We'd all just come from chapel and no one had bothered to turn the lights on and so the only light was like the flicker and glow of all those television screens playing some morning show, do you remember that? It was fucking spooky.

EMILIO. Yeah. I remember it really well.

SIMON. And do you remember you were like, 'We should take pictures?'

EMILIO. Yeah.

SIMON. You were like, 'We should take pictures. We'll win the
Pulitzer Prize.' And we broke into the journalism studio and
stole a couple cameras and we went around taking all these
pictures of these kids in these rooms, their eyes glued to the
screens, with only that blue glow from the TV on their faces,
and the TV host asking somebody, 'Do you think they're going
to fall? They look like they're going to fall?' We hid around
corners and squatted behind bushes because we didn't want
people to see us taking those pictures. The teachers hugging all
the kids who were crying in the hallway whose parents worked
at the Pentagon or whatever. All the people standing on the
field, dialing and redialing on their cellphones. The vice-
principal crying in the car. And then there was that girl on the
courtyard, do you remember that? She told us she'd taken
a Valium and she was laughing and she was like, 'I know I'm
probably going to regret this later, but I can't stop laughing.'
And we took all those pictures of her. We took all those
pictures of her laughing and rolling around in the green under
that totally beautiful day – that clear sky and that sunlight.

EMILIO. Yeah.

SIMON. Whatever happened to those photos?

EMILIO. I actually took them to the drugstore that day to get
developed. But I never picked them up. By the time they were
ready, I was too… embarrassed or something.

SIMON. Yeah… I've never told anyone else about that. Have you?

EMILIO. No.

SIMON. What the fuck were we thinking?

EMILIO. I don't know. I guess. I don't know. I suppose we
thought someone was gonna care about how it felt… to us?
I don't know.

SIMON. Yeah. And now look at all the shit we've been through –
it's like too much, Columbine, 9/11, the war, the war, the war,
then Trump, then COVID, whatever the fuck is going on in the
Supreme Court… Roe v. Wade… I want to say it's too much
for one lifetime, but then I think: what does that even mean?
I look at my parents and I'm like, 'Wait, they lived through all

the same shit and then some?' And don't get me started on my grandparents. I keep asking myself: is this what life is? How did I get it into my head that life was supposed to be something other than this?

The warning sound of EMILIO*'s phone losing power.*

EMILIO. Wait, Simon, fuck, hold on, my phone is about to die and I still have to call a car. Let me go plug it in.

SIMON. Okay.

EMILIO *goes to the door to open it and it's locked.*

EMILIO. Are you fucking kidding me?!

SIMON. What's wrong?

EMILIO. ARE YOU FUCKING KIDDING ME? NO!

SIMON. Emilio? Emilio, what's wr–

The phone dies.

EMILIO. No! No no no no no no no no! I need a car! I NEED A CAR! No!

Blackout.

2.

The porch, hours later. EMILIO *has fallen asleep somewhere slightly hidden. The sound of a car driving up, a door opening, goodbyes being exchanged, and then the car pulling away.* URSULA *enters, carefully making her way to the porch with her white cane, before she sees* EMILIO.

URSULA (*startles*). Oh my God.

Then she sees who it is, approaches and gently wakes EMILIO *up.*

EMILIO. Hmh, wha?

URSULA. Emilio. You scared the crap out of me.

EMILIO. Nguh, tuhh, what time is it? What's going on?

URSULA. It's almost midnight. You've been out here this whole time? It's freezing. I thought you would have gone home.

EMILIO. My phone died before I could call a car. Then I couldn't remember where I was, how to… get around…

URSULA. You didn't want to ask my neighbors for help?

EMILIO. I was going to but… then I got sleepy…

Beat.

What Caitlin said isn't true. I don't think you're –

URSULA. I know you don't.

EMILIO. Then why did you go with her?

URSULA. I was still a little high. It just seemed like the least awkward thing to do. She and Kristina still live here and they've actually been good friends to me. Caitlin loaned me money when I couldn't work. And Kristina's really helpful with doctors. You're lucky. You get to go away. I still have to deal with them.

EMILIO (*harrumphs*). 'Luck.' What is that? Aren't we all lucky? We survived a plague.

Beat.

URSULA. You really hurt them, Emilio.

EMILIO. Well, I feel like I got what I deserved… How was it? Did you have fun?

URSULA. Uh, no. Kristina was so wasted, they nearly asked us to leave. We weren't inside ten minutes before she knocked over an entire platter of salmon and then tried to start picking it up with her bare hands, which got the caterers involved and then she tripped and broke a heel going up to accept the little plaque they were giving out to all the service people, so she spent the rest of the night basically with no shoes on dancing by herself near this poor DJ she kept badgering to play 'MMMBop' before Caitlin got her to sit down and then I babysat her until she passed out.

EMILIO. Wow.

URSULA. Yeah... But people kept asking about you.

EMILIO. Really? What did you say?

URSULA. That you were a fancy international artist living in Berlin with a big show opening up next week in New York. They were impressed.

EMILIO. It sounds impressive.

URSULA. And then, after the fifteenth time of me explaining what had happened to my eye, I learned I wasn't the only diabetic.

EMILIO. Who else?

URSULA. Huey Michael Lewis.

EMILIO. Shut up!

URSULA. I know! Then he and I started talking about it and then suddenly there was this small group of people gathered around sharing all the health crap that was suddenly going on with them – high blood pressure, high cholesterol. Someone had just beat cancer. I guess this is just that age.

EMILIO. The Age of Shit Showing Up.

URSULA. The Age of Bad Choices Seeking Their Consequences. The Comeuppance...

Beat.

Anyway, I kept thinking about what you said earlier, these reunions being like this dark ritual of the soul. I kept thinking, was this what he was talking about? It was, in a weird way kind of nice.

Beat.

Anyway, this new principal came in and shut everything down the way they used to shut the dances down: 'You don't got to go home, but you got to get the heck up out of here.' And everyone went, 'Awww!' And booed like they used to. Even though clearly everyone was ready to go home. It was sweet. For a moment everyone felt like... Like they used to.

EMILIO. Did people think the limo was funny?

URSULA. No. In fact, we spent so much time fucking around on this porch out here that, by the time we pulled up, everyone was already inside. Barely anyone even noticed. And the people that did were… confused…

EMILIO. Hm. And I'm assuming Caitlin left with Paco?

Beat.

URSULA. Nothing's going to happen between them.

EMILIO. Did they leave together or not?

URSULA.…Yes. But Kristina was with them.

EMILIO. Uh-huh. I'm sure they all took a car to Kristina's house, to 'make sure she was okay.' They'll slip her drunk ass in bed and they'll find some quiet place in her house to… Or maybe he'll take her back to his place.

Beat.

URSULA. Why does this matter so much to you?

EMILIO. I don't know. You have no idea how much I wish it didn't. I didn't come back here expecting to feel any of this shit. I'm sort of annoyed that I let it. I'm annoyed that this is all… still part of me…

URSULA. Who cares? Think about your real life, your new life.

EMILIO. What new life? I'm still the same me living the same life.

URSULA. But you have a new baby! You have a partner! Annika!

EMILIO.…Annika's not really my partner.

URSULA. What?

EMILIO. Annika is a friend of mine. She really wanted to have a kid. I did her a favor. Who knows how much I'll actually wind up being in Alena's life? Another thing where I'm like, 'Will I regret this or not?'… No, I won't.

URSULA. Why did you lie?

EMILIO. I don't know. I didn't want to feel... small, or something. I thought it would make me feel bigger. Like I had accomplished something.

Beat.

I've never quite figured out the love thing for myself. There have been a lot of women. Lots of close calls. But nothing ever stuck. I don't know why. I don't know if it's me or not me.

URSULA. I'm sorry.

Beat.

EMILIO. Do you want to marry me?

URSULA. Um...

EMILIO. Come on! I could move back! I could move back here and live here with you! Keep making my art! Take care of you! Come on! We could wake-and-bake all day like you and Grandma, drink whatever you want to make and I'd do the cooking. I've become a very good cook!

URSULA. Well, unfortunately, I am already seeing someone. And it's pretty serious.

EMILIO. What? No you're not. And what's his name?

URSULA. Her name is Lacy. She's the woman who comes and helps me a few times a week? She's actually my girlfriend.

EMILIO *'s mouth falls open.*

EMILIO. Shut the fuck up.

URSULA. What?

EMILIO. You. Are such. A bitch.

URSULA. What!?

EMILIO. Since when have you been dating women!?

URSULA. What do you mean since when? I don't know. College?

EMILIO. How long have you been seeing her?

URSULA. Two years?

EMILIO. And where did you meet?

URSULA. On the apps, obvi.

EMILIO. You are such a little sneak! And wait – why didn't you say something earlier when I was being basically gaybashed!?

URSULA. I don't know. It didn't seem like the right time. It was too tense. She's someone very special to me. And as you know, these people don't know how to mind their own business.

EMILIO. Well, good for you. That's all I have to say. Fucking go get it, Ursula.

Beat.

URSULA. You know, the irony is that all throughout my time with Lacy, I've thought about you.

EMILIO. What?

URSULA. Do you remember the things you used to say about Caitlin freshman year? We would be up late on AOL IMing. You used to just spout all kind of crazy stuff about the way she made you feel. How she came to you in dreams. How you were hearing stupid songs on the radio differently. I remember once you were like, 'I feel like parts of me that have never been awake before are suddenly alive and singing the same song.'

EMILIO (*embarrassed*). Oh God…

URSULA. I loved it! I loved watching you two, watching this drama unfold. But then… I watched you never tell Caitlin how you really felt and one day I realized you were never once going to tell her how you felt and I think you realized that too and you guys just sort of… settled… into this 'best friend' thing and this fairytale died… And then somewhere along the way we had all become M.E.R.G.E.… Then you and Kristina started dating because you felt you kind of had to…

Beat.

You know, I realized only recently how much that that had such an effect on me. I assumed that those feelings, all the things you'd been saying, were just made up. You were such an artist even then. I figured whatever you claimed to be feeling was – I don't know – a lie? A game? A pose.

Beat.

But then came Lacy. And when I'm with her, I feel like parts
of me that have never been awake before are suddenly alive
and singing. I hear all these stupid pop songs on the radio and,
for the first time, I really get – I hear – what they're about.
And I think to myself, how could Emilio have known this if he
hadn't felt them, if they hadn't been real? Those feelings were
real, weren't they?

EMILIO. I don't know. It's like I can remember feeling the
feelings but I can't quite remember the feelings themselves. So
I can't tell you what they are. I can't tell you if they were love
or what. Those feeling are something else now. They're so old.
Those feelings are in their twenties. They can drink now. They
can almost rent a car by themselves. They've got jobs. They've
got advanced degrees. They've got student loans. They've
changed. They've… they've hardened into… something else…
It's just… hard to trust all that stuff you felt. When you were
young. In any case, those feelings weren't reciprocated.

URSULA. I don't think that's true. Why else would she have
trusted you so deeply? Why else would she have handed over
her entire life to you like that?

Beat.

You hide so much, Emilio. You really shouldn't. Your life is
not small.

Beat, before EMILIO *becomes* DEATH.

DEATH. As I was saying, I am here for work, but I will confess it
has been a busier than average few years for me so, as a result,
I have been experimenting with a new approach to things. I've
decided to make it more of a practice to drop by and check in on
people – to check in earlier and check in often. It's a lot more
running around for me but the longer lead time is nice. It's been
helpful to get a better sense of what I'll eventually be walking
into. Fewer surprises. Social gatherings are particularly
convenient – more efficient. More opportunity for multitasking.
More birds, less stones. Working smarter not harder, et cetera.
I really do want the best and most painless ride for everyone.

So I'm actually here for Ursula. She and I are due to meet in
a little under six months. By that point, she will have lost

vision in both of her eyes, so it will be relatively tough for her. This new partner you've just heard about, sensing danger, will wind up fleeing the scene – not an uncommon response, so Ursula will be alone. Nursing both of these losses – of vision and of love – will become too much and Ursula really will evolve into the shut-in Caitlin feared. Melancholy will take root, a deep humiliation. She'll get lost. When she is found, there won't be much clarity. 'It's unclear,' people will whisper, when asked. Her insulin. Was it intentional or had she misplaced it? Or had she merely lost track of the days?

Perhaps you wonder how it is I know all of this? My being in time is somewhat different from yours. My memory extends in all directions. But memory, as you know, is just a myth. Life, the present, is its expression. The present is the best part – of all things. Isn't it. On this side of the veil, at least... This is why I like to watch.

For example: sometime, not too long ago, I sat in some of your kitchens, watching you cooking and eating your meals, wiping down your groceries, trying out new recipes. I sat on the edges of your bed, watching you nod off reading your books, streaming your streams, playing your games on your little devices. I have watched you shit and shower and shave – or not. I saw you bike around empty cities, ride empty trains, take the same walks around the same blocks, talk to neighbors you've never met. I saw you with all this free time, fresh air, no work, staying in one place for weeks and weeks and weeks at a time, living. We never spoke but I could tell you felt me close, that you were thinking of me. Frequently. It was actually kind of nice – not nice to be thought of – or not just that – but nice to see you so... thoughtful, so different. For some reason you were much kinder and, somehow, awake. You helped each other, even if that meant just washing your hands a little more or chanting in the streets. I don't know what it was – but for the first time, I'll confess, in a long time, I thought you were the best versions of yourselves – or at least the ones I've seen. Man, was it easy to... root for you. Tell me, did you feel it? Or was I just making it up? You all were much more... likeable? Is that the word? Your character was much more likeable... what happened?

Beat, no response.

You know what? Think on that. You can tell me later.

EMILIO *becomes* EMILIO *again.*

EMILIO. Can I see your phone?

EMILIO *gets up and turns on the Bluetooth speaker from earlier.*

URSULA. Oh no. More dancing?

URSULA *hands it over and* EMILIO *connects the phone to the speakers.*

EMILIO. No. I want to show you something.

URSULA. Show me what?

EMILIO. You asked me earlier about my piece in New York, how the sounds work. I use these things called mosquito tones.

URSULA. Mosquito tones?

EMILIO. Yeah. They're these sounds that are like right on the edge of your hearing range, but only certain people of certain ages can hear certain ones, because as you get older and older, your range of hearing gets narrower and narrower.

URSULA. Oh. Interesting.

EMILIO. Obviously, we don't have any speakers hidden in walls, so I can't give you a spatial experience, but I can try to paint a picture for you. Here's the first tone. Just keep pressing that button. And every time you press it, imagine you're moving further and further into a long white hall that stretches for as far as you can see, and when you can't hear anything, that's where you stop, okay?

URSULA. Okay.

Beats, as they move through several tones.

EMILIO. Okay. We just passed the edge of my hearing range.

URSULA.... Really?

EMILIO. Yeah. I can't hear anything anymore... Can you?

Lights begin to fade.

URSULA. Yeah, I can still hear something…

Beat.

I think…

Blackout.

End of Play.